ANNALS

of the

TOWN OF CONCORD

IN THE COUNTY OF MERRIMACK, AND STATE OF NEW HAMPSHIRE,
FROM ITS FIRST SETTLEMENT, IN THE YEAR 1726,
TO THE YEAR 1823.

WITH SEVERAL BIOGRAPHICAL SKETCHES.

TO WHICH IS ADDED,

A Memoir of the Penacook Indians

By
Jacob B. Moore

"Let us read, and recollect, and impress upon our souls, the views and ends of our forefathers, in exchanging their native country for a dreary, inhospitable wilderness. Recollect their amazing fortitude, their bitter sufferings! the hunger, the nakedness, the cold, which they patiently endured! the severe labors of clearing their grounds, building their houses, and raising their provisions, amidst dangers from wild beasts and savage men." – ADAMS.

HERITAGE BOOKS
2024

HERITAGE BOOKS

AN IMPRINT OF HERITAGE BOOKS, INC.

Books, CDs, and more—Worldwide

For our listing of thousands of titles see our website
at
www.HeritageBooks.com

A Facsimile Reprint
Published 2024 by
HERITAGE BOOKS, INC.
Publishing Division
5810 Ruatan Street
Berwyn Heights, MD 20740

Concord:
Published by Jacob B. Moore
1824

Cover Illustration: South-East View of the Capitol.

International Standard Book Number
Paperbound: 978-0-7884-9530-4

PREFACE.

WHEN the compilation of the following brief notices was undertaken, the writer had no other intention than to preserve the facts which he might obtain for his own particular use and amusement.—But on examination, many things of an interesting nature were found mingled with the concerns of the town, which it was conceived might be useful and entertaining to the inhabitants. The circumstances attending the first settlement, the hardships endured by the settlers, and their frequent exposure to Indian warfare ; the massacre by the Indians, and their depredations upon the property of the inhabitants ; and the tedious and perplexing controversy with the proprietors of Bow—were all deemed subjects of sufficient importance to interest the people of this town. The generation to whom these things were familiar, is rapidly passing away ; and there will ere long be no one, from whom these particulars could be collected. Even at this time, great difficulty has been encountered in connecting the series of events, and reconciling contradictory accounts. The want of records, for several years, and the deficiency of a portion of those we have, were also evils not to be remedied but by unwearied search and inquiry among the most intelligent aged people of the town. The writer has devoted much time to the collection of the materials here embodied ; and though, from the nature of things, and his own inability to give the narrative any original attractions, he must be aware that errors and deficiencies may be discovered—it is believed the good citizens of Concord will find some things, embraced in the following pages, worthy of perusal and of preservation.

For the memoir of the tribe of Indians, who once inhabited this town and vicinity, the writer acknowledges his obligations to John Farmer, Esq. of this town. To the politeness of Charles Walker, and Francis N. Fisk, Esquires, and the Rev. Dr. M'Farland, he is also indebted for the use of sundry records and papers in their possession, which have been of great service to him. And to the aged citizens generally who have cheerfully aided him in completing this task, would he present the most hearty thanks, with the hope that what they have helped to accomplish, will not be found so wholly uninteresting as to be deemed unworthy of preservation.

March 1, 1824.

ANNALS OF CONCORD.

—·)●◉●(·—

CONCORD, the seat of the state government, and shire town of the county of Merrimack, New-Hampshire, is pleasantly situated on both sides of Merrimack river, in latitude 43° 12′ N.; 45 miles N. 72½° W. of Portsmouth, 62 miles N. 22° W. of Boston, and 500 miles from Washington-City. It was originally known by the name of *Penacook*, from that of the tribe of Indians who once inhabited the vicinity. It is bounded on the north-west by Canterbury and Boscawen, north-east by Loudon and Chichester, south-east by Pembroke and Bow, and south-west by Hopkinton: comprising an area of 40,919 acres.

As the principal design of this little work is to present in a summary view the most interesting circumstances which can now be collected in relation to the history of Concord, further notice of its local situation, topography, &c. will be omitted in this place.

In the settlement of new lands, emigrants have generally been careful to select such as were fertile, and well situated for their various pursuits. Hence alluvial valleys and the borders of rivers are sooner settled than the highlands, which, though often as productive, are less easy of cultivation. The Indians were not less sagacious in this particular than the whites, for we find near our principal rivers, remains of their fortifications, and other memorials of their residence there. The intervals situated on the river Merrimack early attracted notice; and several parties, desirous of commencing new settlements, surveyed the lands a great distance from its mouth.

About the year 1720, Captain Ebenezer Eastman and several others, from Haverhill, Mass. explored the lands in this vicinity, and noticing the
richness of the intervals, resolved to procure a
grant and commence a settlement. Accordingly,
at the session of the "General Court of the Province of the Massachusetts Bay," assembled at Boston in May, 1721, a petition was presented for a
tract of land "situated on the river Merrymake, at
the lower end of Penacook," to contain about eight
miles square. The petitioners were unsuccessful
in their application until 1725; the governor dis-
senting from all proceedings of the legislature,
though they twice "allowed the petition," in 1721
and 1722, and in 1724 appointed a committee to
view the lands. In the beginning of the year 1725,
upon the petition of Benjamin Stevens, Ebenezer
Eastman and others, in behalf of the intended settlers, a tract of land of about seven miles square
was appropriated for a township, by the government of Massachusetts. The conditions of the
grant were, that the tract should be divided into
one hundred and three equal shares or lots; that
one hundred families should settle thereon within
the space of three years; that each settler should
build a good dwelling-house, "comfortably to receive and entertain his family," and break up and
fence in six acres of land for a home lot, within
the term aforesaid; that the houses should be

1725. *Jan.* 18. At a meeting of the committee of the general court of Massachusetts, for bringing forward the settlement of a place called Penacook, on each
side of Merrimack river, to begin where Contoocook empties itself into the Merrimack—present William Tailor, Elisha Cooke, William Dudley, John Wainwright, Captain John Shapleigh, John Sanders, Eleazar Tyng, and Mr. Joseph
Wilder—each admitted settler paid the committee 20s.

Feb. 7. "Voted that the settlers shall well and truly fulfil the conditions and orders of the general court. And for the effectual accomplishing the same, it is agreed
and resolved, that such and so many of the intended settlers as shall fail of fallowing,
fencing or clearing one acre of land within twelve months from the first of June
next, shall each of them forfeit and pay the community or settlers, £5, to be appropriated by them to their own benefit."—*Pro. Records.*

erected within twenty rods of each other on the home lots, and in a regular and defensible manner; and that a convenient house for the public worship of God should be completely finished within the time first mentioned. Each settler was to pay the province £5 for his right; and as soon as one hundred were admitted settlers, they were empowered to hold proprietary meetings for the transaction of the business of the settlement. The remaining three rights were reserved, one for the first settled minister, one for a parsonage, and one for " the use of the school forever."* The requisite number of settlers having been admitted, a meeting was holden at Haverhill, on the 7th of February, 1725, when the following, among other regulations, was adopted by the proprietors:

" *Agreed and resolved*, That no alienation on any
" lot shall be made without the consent of the com-
" munity. And if any of the intended settler or
" settlers shall alienate his or their lots or settle-
" ments to any person or persons, without the con-
" sent of the community first had and obtained, such
" sale shall be declared void of itself, and the
" settler that shall so pretend to alienate his lot,
" shall forfeit the same to the community."†

The object of this regulation undoubtedly was to exclude *Irish settlers*, against whom a strong national prejudice existed, heightened perhaps by zeal in differing religious opinions. There is another evidence of this in the last petition,

1726. At a meeting of the "intended settlers," at Andover, Feb. 8, it was agreed and voted that a block house of 25 feet in breadth and 40 feet in length be built at Penacook, for the security of the settlers.

—— *June* 28. Mr. Agent Dummer, at London, was instructed, as it was apprehended by the government of Massachusetts, that New-Hampshire might send home a complaint against the grant of Penacook lately made, to take care and answer any complaint; and he was furnished with the necessary papers.—*Mass. Records.*

* See Appendix No. I.
† For the names of the original proprietors, see Appendix No. II.

by Stevens and others : They state, " that ma-
" ny applications have been made to the govern-
" ment of New-Hampshire for a grant of the said
" land, (at Penacook) which, though it be the un-
" doubted right and property of this province ; yet
" it is highly probable that *a parcel of Irish people*
" will obtain a grant from New-Hampshire for it,
" unless some speedy care be taken by this great
" and honorable court to prevent it."*

In May, 1726, a committee appointed by the
government of Massachusetts, with surveyors,
chainmen, and a number of the admitted settlers
attending them, " proceeded to Penacook, and laid
out 103 home lots or divisions on the river, in equal
proportion, according to the quantity and quality,
as near as the land would admit thereof, agreeabl
to the order and direction of the great and genera!
court."† This year considerable progress was made

---

*The jealousy prevalent at this period of the encroachments of settlers upon un
appropriated lands, is also evinced in the following order of the general court o
Massachusetts, relative to the settlers of Nutfield, [Londonderry] passed Dec. 1
1720 :

" Whereas it appears that several familys lately arrived from Ireland, and other
from this province, have presumed to make a settlement upon lands belonging to
this province, lying westward of the town of Haverhill, (which they call Nutfield
without any leave or grant obtained from this court : *Resolved*, that the said peopl
be warned to move off from said lands, within the space of seven months, and i
they fail to do so, that they be prosecuted by the Attorney-General by writts of tres-
pass and ejectment."

† *Extracts from the journal kept by John Wainwright, one of the committee.*

May 12, 1726. The committee left Haverhill, and proceeded as far as Amos-
keag.

13*th*. " This morning we proceeded on our journey—very hilly and mountainous land. About 8 o'clock we passed by a fall called *Annahookline*, [Hooksett] in
Merrimack river, which is taken from a hill of the same name. About 10 or 11
o'clock, we forded Suncook river, which is a rapid stream, and many loose stones
of some considerable bignesse in it, making it difficult to pass. About 1 o'clock
we passed Penacook river, [Soucook] pretty deep and very rocky In a short time
after, we came up as far as Penacook falls, [Garven's] and steered our course north
over a large pitch pine plain, three miles at least in length, and about 5 o'clock afternoon arrived at Penacook, and encamped on a piece of intervale called Sugar-
Ball plain, from a very large head or hill called Sugar-Ball hill, whereon was the
first Indian fort, as we were informed, which the Indians in old times built to defend
themselves against the Maquois [Mohawks] and others their enemies. This Sugar-
Ball plain is a pretty large tract of land encompassed on all parts with very high
and mountainous land, as steep as the roof of an house ordinarily—only where
the river runs round it, which encompasses the other parts of it. It is altogether
impracticable for a team or even horse-cart to get on the plain, the land is so mountainous round it ; and there is no spring on it as we could find."

14*th*. " About 12 o'clock this day, Messrs. Nathaniel Weare, Richard Waldron,
jun. and Theodore Atkinson, a committee appointed by the governor and council of

in the settlement, about fifty persons being employed during the warmer season. A new path was cut through the woods from Haverhill to Penacook, by the way of Chester, some portion of the distance on the same route now travelled. The same year the building of a block-house, for the defence of the plantation, and also to serve for a place of public worship, was commenced—to be 25 feet in breadth and 40 in length.

New-Hampshire,came up to our camp, (being attended with about half a score Irishmen, who kept at some distance from the camp) and acquainted us that the government of New-Hampshire, being informed of our business here, had sent them to desire us that we would not proceed in appropriating these lands to any private or particular persons, for that they lay in their government; and our government's making a grant might be attended with very ill consequences to the settlers, when it appeared that the lands fell in the N. H. government. And then they delivered a copy of an order passed by his honour the lieutenant governor and council of New-Hampshire respecting the settling of the lands at Penacook,to which we refer. We made them answer, that the government of the Massachusetts Bay had sent us to lay out the lands here into a township; that they had made a grant of it to some particular men, and that we should proceed to do the business we were come upon, and made no doubt but our government would be always ready to support and justifie their own grants; and that it was the business of the publick, and not ours, to engage in, in order to determine any controversy about the lands. We sent our salutes to the lieutenant governor of New-Hampshire, and the gentlemen took their leaves of us, and set homewards this afternoon."

15th. "SUNDAY.—Mr. Enoch Coffin, our chaplain, performed divine service both parts of the day."

16th. "At sunrise this morning, according to notification, we chose a representative, nem. con. viz. Mr. John Sanders."

18th. "It may be observed, that divers rattlesnakes were killed by the several surveying companies, but, thanks be to God, nobody received any hurt from them."

The committee in their report, (June, 1726) say,—"In May last, we proceeded to the place, in order to lay out the whole township, and the lots directed in the order of the General Court, beginning at the mouth of Contoocook river, where that joins Merrimack river, and thence run a line east seventeen degrees south four miles, and so at right angles at the extremes of each of the aforesaid lines, seven miles southerly each, and thence from the termination of the seven miles which completes the grant and is according thereto; and upon view and strict survey of the lands on the east side of Merrimack, we find that there is little or no water, the land near the river extremely mountainous and almost impassable, and very unfit for and uncapable of receiving fifty families, as the court has ordered; more especially considering that near the centre of the town on the east side of the river Merrimack, the Hon. Samuel Sewall, Esq. has a farm of five hundred acres of good land, formerly granted by this court, and laid out by Gov. Endicott. The committee, therefore, with submission to the honorable General Court, thought it advisable and accordingly have laid out one hundred and three lots of land for settlements, on the west side contiguous to each other, regularly, and in a defensible manner, as by the plot of theirs, and of the whole grant (which is hereby presented) will appear; and inasmuch as the generality of the land answers not the grantees' expectation, and five hundred acres laid out as aforesaid, humbly offer, that the like number of acres of the unappropriated lands adjacent to the township, may be made to the settlers as an equivalent therefor." The government of Massachusetts thereupon empowered the grantees to make settlements on the westerly side of the river at pleasure.

The Indians who at this time inhabited the vicinity, were on terms of amity with the whites.
During the winter of this year, two or three persons only resided in the block-house at Penacook.
The snow was very deep, the cold unusually severe,
and their provisions were insufficient to support
them through the season. The Indians saw
their situation, and as soon as possible journeyed
to Haverhill. They there called on the proprietors, and represented to them the situation of the
families, very seriously observing that *they would
soon come upon the town*, unless they were assisted!
A sleigh with stores soon after arrived at Penacook,
and rescued them from starvation.

On the 20th May, 1727, the government of New-
Hampshire made a grant to Jonathan Wiggin and
others of the tract comprised within the following
bounds, viz : " beginning on the S. E. side of the
town of Chichester, and running nine miles by Chichester and Canterbury, and carrying that breadth
of nine miles from each of the aforesaid towns
S. W. until the full complement of eighty-one square
miles are fully made up." This grant, covering the
greater part both of Concord and Pembroke, and a
part of Hopkinton, gave rise to a serious controversy between the claimants under each grant, which
was continued in law for several years, and was not
finally settled until 1762.

During the year 1727, the block-house was finished; considerable quantities of corn and hay were
gathered, and the wilderness reduced to some de-

1726. *Dec.* 20. The memorial of the Penacook settlers was presented, respecting
500 acres of land on the E. side of the river, formerly granted to Gov. Endicott,
and praying for land instead thereof on the W. Voted unanimously to grant 500
acres on the west side. This grant was confirmed by governor Burnet, Aug. 6,
1728.—*Mass. Records.*

1727. *March* 6. Messrs. Joseph Hall and John Pecker were "empowered to
to agree with a minister to preach at Penacook the year ensuing, to begin the service from the fifteenth of May next. The said committee are directed to act with
all prudence, and not assure the gentleman more than after the rate of £100 per
annum for his service."—*Prop. Records.*

gree of cultivation. Several dwellings had previously been erected; and in the fall of this year the first family, that of Ebenezer Eastman, moved into the place.*

Aug. 6, 1728, the government of Massachusetts, in consideration of a grant of 500 acres of land, formerly made to governor Endicott, which fell within the boundaries of Penacook, and was claimed by the heirs of judge Sewall, empowered the proprietors "by a surveyor and chainmen on oath, to extend the south bounds of the township one hundred rods the full breadth of their town, as an equivalent."

Considerable improvements were made in the settlements in 1729 ; saw and gristmills were erected by Nathan Simonds, with the assistance of the proprietors ; and a ferry was established for the convenience of the settlers.† A substantial fence was this year built for the first time to enclose the interval on the river, "at the common charge." A

1728. On the 15th of February this year, the first child was born at Penacook—Dorcas, a daughter of Edward and Dorcas Abbot: she died Sept. 28, 1797. The first male child was Edward, son of the same parents, born Dec. 27, 1730: he died in Sept. 1801. John Hoit, the second male, was born Sept. 10, 1732—and married a sister of Dr. Carter, Jan. 2, 1755. The elder Mr. Hoit was of Amesbury, Ms.

1729. Sept. 4. The proprietors and inhabitants of Penacook petitioned the general court of Massachusetts for the privileges of a town ; but no proceedings were had. March 6, 1730, the same petition was renewed, and referred to the consideration of a committee ; but no measures were adopted.

* Jacob Shute drove Eastman's team, the first that had crossed the wilderness from Haverhill to Penacook. Shute's father was a native of France, and upon the revocation of the Edict of Nantz by Lewis XIV. fled into Ireland. His children emigrated to this country.

Though Eastman's was the first *family* of settlers, it is believed there were several individuals who settled previously. Dr. Rolfe was the first settler, and resided near the residence of the late captain Emery. He was father of Benjamin Rolfe, Esq. The second settler was Richard Uran, afterwards of Newbury. They passed the winter of 1726 at Penacook, living mostly upon the fruits of the wilderness and the *charities* of the Indians.

† The gristmill stood near the present site of the factory of Messrs. I. & J. Eastman, on the east side of the river ; the saw-mill about half a mile above, on the same stream. The mill-crank was brought upon a horse from Haverhill. Soon after commencing operations, it was broken. How to remedy the evil they knew not, as there was no blacksmith nearer than Haverhill. But necessity is the mother of invention. They collected together a quantity of pitch knots, fastened the crank with beetle-rings and wedges, and succeeded in their attempt to weld the disjointed parts. The crank was afterwards used for many years.

plank floor was also laid in the "meeting-house," or fort; and the road from Penacook to Haverhill, was altered and improved under the direction of Messrs. Ebenezer Eastman and John Chandler.

The settlers of Penacook, like those of all the older towns, strictly observed the religious institutions of their fathers. Mr. Enoch Coffin, of Newbury, Mass. accompanied them on their first visits to the new lands, and other clergymen occasionally preached to them.* Measures were this year taken to provide for the settlement of a minister; and at a meeting of the settlers in October, it was "voted that every proprietor or intended settler of Penacook should forthwith pay or cause to be paid into the hands of the treasurer the sum of 20s. towards the support of an orthodox minister to preach at Penacook aforesaid, the same to be paid in proportion to the preaching." At a previous meeting, they had appointed Deacon John Osgood, Messrs. John Pecker, John Chandler, Ebenezer Eastman, Nathan Symonds, William Barker and Joseph Hall "to call† and agree with some suitable person to be minister of the town of Penacook;" and at the same meeting agreed to pay a salary of £100 lawful money per annum to their minister when settled.‡

---

* At a meeting of the proprietors, at Bradford, March 12, 1728, they voted to pay Mr. Bezaliel Toppan 30s. " for preaching and performing divine service at Penacook." £4 was also voted to the heirs of Rev. Enoch Coffin, deceased, for like services. Mr. Enoch Coffin, the first preacher in Concord, was born in Newbury, Feb. 7, 1695, and died Aug. 7, 1727. He was second son of the honorable Nathaniel Coffin, and graduated at Harvard College. Nathaniel was son of Tristram Coffin, of Newbury, whose father Tristram Coffin was son of Peter Coffin, of Brixton parish, 4 miles from Plymouth in Plympton hundred, and who came to New England in 1642, and brought with him his mother, two sisters, and four children.

† The mode of calling and maintaining ministers in congregational societies, originated in an act passed during the reign of William and Mary, approved June 8, 1692.—*Act IV. William & Mary.*

‡ At the meeting of the grantees and settlers, October 14, 1730, it was " *Voted,* that Mr. Timothy Walker shall have £100 for the year ensuing, and then rise 40s. per annum, till it comes to £120, and that to be the stated sum annually for his salary, during his continuance in the ministry, together with the parsonage so long as he carries on the whole work of the ministry. Provided, and it is hereby to be understood, any thing to the contrary above mentioned notwithstanding, that if Mr. Walker, by *extreme old age,* shall be disenabled from carrying on the whole work of the ministry, that he shall abate so much of his salary as shall be rational."

The inhabitants, at a meeting in March, 1730, instructed the committee before named to invite Mr. Timothy Walker, a graduate of Cambridge, who had just finished his theological studies, to settle with them. On the 14th of October, the proprietors renewed this invitation; and established the salary for the year ensuing at £100, to be increased £2 yearly until it should amount to £120 per annum, which, together with the use of the parsonage, should thereafter constitute the emoluments of their minister. £100 were also voted as a settlement. To the invitation of the people, Mr. Walker returned the following answer:

"*Penacook, Oct.* 14, 1730.

"To the admitted settlers or grantees of Penacook.

"Whereas formerly by a committee you have invited me to settle in the ministry in the said township, upon which invitation I have advised with learned, pious and judicious divines in the ministry, who have jointly advised me to take up with your invitation, provided you vote a sufficient maintenance for me; and you having this day renewed your invitation to me, and done what satisfies me upon the account of salary:—I therefore, being deeply sensible of the importance of the charge, and my own insufficiency to discharge the duties of the same, do accept your call, humbly relying upon the all-sufficient grace of God, which alone can enable me suitably to discharge the same, earnestly desiring your prayers, as well as all others of God's people, that such plentiful measures of His grace may be afforded to me, as may enable me to discharge the duties of so sacred a function, to his acceptance and your edification;

1730. *Oct.* 14.—Voted, that Mr. Cutting Noyes have fifty acres of land in the township of Penacook—provided the said Noyes shall do the *blacksmith's work* of the town from the date hereof.—*Prop. Records.*

3

that so both you and I may rejoice together in the day of the Lord Jesus.

TIMOTHY WALKER."

The ordination of Rev. Mr. Walker took place on the 18th of November following. The sermon was delivered by the Rev. John Barnard,[*] of Andover, Mass. ; charge by Rev. Samuel Phillips, of Andover ; and right hand of fellowship by the Rev. John Brown, of Haverhill. The church was composed of sober and industrious inhabitants ; and during the whole course of Mr. Walker's ministry, we do not find that any dissentions or difficulties arose. The people were united in interests and feelings, were educated in the same principles, and generally adopted like habits ; and perhaps all strictly united in one mode of worship, and were constant in the observance of religious ordinances.

The meeting-house was this year repaired ; and the first burial-place in Concord located and enclosed. The first bridge in the township was built over Soucook river. By an order of the general court of Massachusetts, founded upon a petition of the proprietors, they were empowered to exercise the privileges and immunities of a town in the assessment and collection of taxes, &c. But from some imperfection in the order itself, or some other cause, it was not made use of.

Jan. 31st, 1731, the petition of the inhabitants, &c. of Penacook was renewed, praying for town privileges, and representing that there were then in the settlement eighty families. February 1, a report was made in favor of the petitioners, accepted, and the act accordingly passed.

The first legal meeting of " the inhabitants of the plantation of Penacook," was holding at the meeting-house, Jan. 11, 1732. Capt. Ebenezer

---

[*]There is this *peculiar circumstance* in your settlement,that *it is* in a place,where *Satan,* some years ago, had his seat, and the *devil* was wont to be *Invocated* by forsaken *Salvages :* A Place which was the *Rendezvous* and *Head Quarters* of our *Indian Enemies."*— *Barnard's Sermon, p.* 29.

Eastman was appointed moderator ; and the necessary town officers were chosen "to stand to the an-
niversary meeting in March" following. This
meeting was called by "Benjamin Rolfe, by order
of the General Court." In the afternoon of the
same day, after a notice for that purpose had been
issued by the new authorities of Penacook, the inhabitants voted to raise £110 for the support of the
ordained minister. At the next meeting, on the 6th
of March, besides choosing town officers, the inhabitants voted a bounty of 20s. for every wolf
"killed within the township;" also a bounty of 6d.
for killing rattle-snakes, "provided, that the des-
troyer of such snakes shall bring in a black
joint of the tail or with the tail to the selectmen, or
either of them." A penny was also voted "for
the encouragement of killing of black-birds within
the township for the year ensuing, the head being
brought to the selectmen or any of them, and burnt."
The proprietors this year appropriated 100 acres,
including the privileges on Turkey river, to "any
suitable person who would build a grist mill."

In 1733, the "plantation of Penacook" was incorporated by the government of Massachusetts as
a town by the name of *Rumford*, it being satisfacto-
rily ascertained, as set forth in the preamble to the
act, that "the plantation is competently filled with
inhabitants, who have built and finished a convenient meeting-house for the public worship of God,
and sometime since have settled a learned orthodox minister among them," &c. This name was
given from that of a parish in England. The town
at their several meetings this year, voted to give
Rev. Mr. Walker £50, for building him a dwelling-
house, provided that he gave the inhabitants and
freeholders a receipt in full for his salary until the
16th of January that year, in consequence of the
depreciation of money, it not being equal to silver
at 17s. the ounce. £30 were appropriated of the
monies in the town treasury for the purchase of am-

munition for the use of the inhabitants. It appears that some fears were entertained of the hostile disposition of the Indians, although no act of aggression had been committed. The sum of £16 was also voted for the support of a school during the winter and spring ensuing ; and the selectmen were empowered to provide a school. It was also voted in town meeting that the selectmen should " find books for the use of the inhabitants and freeholders of the town or plantation, on the town's cost, so far as they shall think necessary." Mr. James Scales, afterwards minister at Hopkinton, was employed to teach the first school; and after him, Mr. Joseph Holt, of Andover, Mass.

From this period until 1739, the affairs of the town continued to prosper with little interruption. Some useful internal regulations were adopted—improvements on the lands were constantly making—the meeting-house was further repaired—and increased attention was paid to the school. In 1735, also, a committee was appointed to petition government for the establishment of a new county, the county of Essex then comprehending all the new grants made by Massachusetts north of Haverhill.

1734. *May* 27.—" 20s. for each grown wolf," and " 1s. for each rattlesnake, which should be killed this year, were voted. At a meeting holden the 14th Nov. of the same year, Capt. Ebenezer Eastman and Henry Rolfe, Esq. were chosen to petition the General Court for an order of said Court for raising of money for defraying the ministerial charge, and the other charges of this town for this year and during the court's pleasure."

At the next town meeting, holden on the 26th day of December, £110 were raised for said purpose. The town clerk was also empowered to " ask and receive of John Wainwright, Esq. the clerk of the honorable committee of the Great and General Court, appointed to bring forward the settlement of the township, the book of the proceedings of the said committee, and all the other papers belonging to the town and proprietors," and to receipt for them. Wainwright had for several years been clerk to the proprietors of Penacook. Some disagreement arising, they appointed another in his stead, to whom he refused to deliver the records. Nor was the matter compromised until Wainwright received from the proprietors an entire lot of land in the new township—upon which he gave up the records to his successor. The grant was made June 19, 1734.

In 1737, the controversy between Massachusetts and New-Hampshire was heard before commissioners appointed by the Crown. Many attempts had previously been made without success to settle it. New-Hampshire took its name from grants made by the council of Plymouth to Capt. John Mason. Of these there had been four or five, all containing more or less of the same lands. Exceptions being taken to all of them, the controversy had turned upon the construction of the Massachusetts charters. At a hearing before the king in council, in 1677, the agents of Massachusetts, by advice, disclaimed jurisdiction beyond the three miles north of Merrimack river specified in the original charter—and it was determined they had right as far as the river extended; but how far it did extend was not expressly mentioned. It seems, however, not to have been doubted—and soon after the government was transferred from Old England to New, it was known by the name of Merrimack as

At the meeting March 11, 1734, the necessary town officers were chosen, and some highway regulations adopted. The premiums on wolves and rattlesnakes were continued.

1735. At a meeting of the "inhabitants and freeholders of the town of Rumford on the 19th of May, 1735, it was put to vote by the moderator, whether they would choose a representative or not, and it passed in the negative." Benjamin Rolfe, Esq. was constituted attorney in behalf of the town to sue the treasurer, John Chandler, for monies not paid over to the town. At the next meeting, holden on the 22d Sept. of the same year, " about £62 were raised for schooling and building part of a bridge over Soucook river," and defraying other expences of the town. A committee was empowered to hire a school-master for four months "the next winter and spring."

A meeting was called on the 10th of December of this year, and a committee appointed to superintend the building of the bridge over the Soucook, and see that the work was "done well and faithfully." At the annual meeting holden March 9, this year, £50 were granted Rev. Mr. Walker "to enable him to clear a pasture and to bring it to English grass," 30l. of which was to be paid in 1736, and the remaining 20l. in 1737. 10s. bounty on wolves and the same sum on rattlesnakes, continued. Henry Rolfe, Esq. was "chosen and desired to assist and join with others that are or may be chosen for to use proper means for to get the county of Essex divided into two counties." The seats in the meeting-house were ordered to be repaired, a door made for the pulpit, and the windows put up.

far as Penacook. If the original charter of Massachusetts had continued, it is not probable any different construction would ever have been started. But in the new charter, the boundary was differently expressed, and a construction was given which made the line to commence 3 miles north of the mouth of the Merrimack, and run west to the South sea, or the other possessions of the King.

About this time, the government of Massachusetts made grants of several towns between Merrimack and Connecticut rivers—amongst the rest, Penacook, &c. And the government of New-Hampshire supposed that Massachusetts was taking this step in order to strengthen their title by possession. After some delay, commissioners were appointed to settle the line, and met at Hampton, N. H. on the 1st of August, 1737. Mr. Livingston of New-York, presided. After many weeks spent in hearing parties and evidence, and having doubts whether the Massachusetts new charter comprehended the whole of the old colony, they made a decree, with contingencies, subject to the determination of the King. The agents of both governments were active at the British court—and a patient hearing was had, though the judgment of the commissioners was for some reason entirely laid aside. It was determined there that the northern boundaries of Massachusetts should be a line three miles from the river as far as Pawtucket falls, thence west to the New-York line.*

1736. At the annual meeting in March, the usual business was transacted, and some improvements in highways, &c. agreed upon. There was also a meeting holden May 18th, same year, called for the purpose of choosing a " person to represent them at the Great and General Court to be held at the town house in Boston," on the 26th next then following ; but the people declined electing.

1737. It appears by warrants recorded that a town meeting was holden in March of 1737, but its proceedings are not on record. At the meeting holden May 16th following, the town again declined sending a representative to the General Court. It does not appear that any other business was transacted.

* Hutch. Mass. vol. ii. p. 342—350.

The inhabitants at a meeting in 1739, ordered a garrison to be built around Rev. Timothy Walker's dwelling-house. £5 were also granted Mr. Barachias Farnum, to enable him to build a flanker in order to defend his mills, on condition that he should garrison his own dwelling-house. Their apprehensions were now increasing of an attack from the Indians, who inhabited the wilds on the north and west, especially as strong parties of them had visited different places within a few days march, and some offences had been committed. No disasters, however, happened to the inhabitants of Rumford until the fatal attack in 1746.

On the 11th of June, 1740, in pursuance of a precept from the Government of Massachusetts, the first representative from the town of Rumford (*Benjamin Rolfe, Esq.*) was elected. His instructions were to prefer a petition to his Majesty that the inhabitants " may be quieted in their posses-" sions, and remain under the jurisdiction of the " Massachusetts Bay; also to petition the General " Court to use their influence with his Majesty in " in that behalf." At a meeting in September, " the " town being informed that by the determination of " his Majesty in Council respecting the controvert-" ed bounds between the province of Massachusetts

1738. The annual meeting for 1738 was on the 29th March. Galleries to the meeting-house were ordered to be built, and other repairs to be made ; also the burying ground to be fenced. The town again, at their meeting 24th May this year, refused sending a representative.

1739. At the meeting in March, it was voted that a school be kept within this town from the 20th Oct. till 20th of April 1740. A meeting was holden Nov. 7th this year; when it was voted that there should be " a good and sufficient garrison built around the Rev. Mr. Timothy Walker's dwelling house as soon as may be conveniently, at the town's cost." 5*l* were also granted to Mr. Barachias Farnum to enable him to build a flanker in order to defend his mills, provided the said Farnum shall give security to the town that in case he shall not keep a garrison at his dwelling house, the town shall have liberty to take said flanker and convert it to their own use." Another meeting was holden on the 28th Dec. of this year, and a committee appointed to inform of all breaches and prosecute for viola:. tions of the act for the preservation of Deer, &c.

" Bay and New-Hampshire, they were excluded
" from the former province, to which they always
" supposed themselves to belong—voted unani-
" mously, to prefer a petition to the King's most
" excellent Majesty, setting forth their distressed
" estate, and praying to be annexed to the said
" Massachusetts province."

By an act of the General Assembly of New-
Hampshire, passed March 18, 1741–2, Rumford
was made a distinct parish or district, and authorized for six years to exercise certain necessary corporate privileges.

The first school-house in this town was erected
in 1742. About this time, the wife of Mr. Jonathan
Eastman was taken prisoner by a party of Indians,
and carried to Canada. She was soon after redeemed by her husband, and returned to her family.

The opening of the French war in 1744, caused
a general anxiety throughout the colonies, and particularly on the frontiers most exposed to Indian
depredations. Gov. Wentworth, in his message to
the General Assembly in May of this year, exhorts
them " to consider with great tenderness the dis-
" tress the inhabitants on the frontiers are in at
" this juncture, and to make their unhappy situation
" their own : to consider them as every day expos-
" ed to a surprize from the enemy," and that if
provisions for their safety were neglected, they
would " become an easy prey to a cruel and bar-
" barous enemy." Measures were accordingly

1742. The annual meeting this year was on the 31st March. Messrs. Edward Abbot, John Merrill and Nathaniel Abbot were directed " to take care and build a
school-house for this town, as they shall in their best judgment think best—the said
house to be built between the widow Barker's barn and the brook by the clay-
pits."

1744. On the 28th March, the meeting for choice of officers, &c. was holden this
year. 20s. O. T. for each wolf, and 2s. O. T. for each rattlesnake were voted to be
allowed for this year. A vote passed granting liberty for such persons as chose to
hire a mistress to use the school-house, until the town had occasion therefor. On
the 21st Jan. B. Rolfe was elected to represent the district of Rumford in the Gen.
Assembly at Portsmouth.

taken for the safety of those towns most exposed, and small detachments were ordered to the aid of the settlements at Canterbury and Contoocook, (now Boscawen.) The inhabitants of Rumford were as yet without military succour, and they empowered Benjamin Rolfe to petition the legislature of New-Hampshire " for such a number of soldiers as " might be sufficient with the divine blessing to de- " fend them against all attempts of their enemies." His petition* was presented in June, of that year, but no detachment was ordered out. In December, the inhabitants again authorized Mr. Rolfe to peti-tion the General Assembly of this province for aid ; and also " to represent to his Excellency the Gov- " ernor and General Court of the province of the " Massachusetts Bay, their deplorable circumstan- " ces, being exposed to imminent danger both from " the French and Indian enemy, and to request of " them such aids as to their great wisdom should " seem meet, and which might be sufficient to ena- " ble them with a divine blessing vigorously to re- " pel all attempts of their enemies." Like peti-tions were also presented in 1745, and a detach-ment of men was stationed here from Billerica, for a few weeks, by direction of the government of Massachusetts.

On Friday, the 7th of August, 1746, a party of In dians from Canada, to the number of about one hund-red, came into this town, and meditated the destruc-tion of the place on the Sabbath following. The in-habitants had for some time previous been expect-ing an attack, and had made an earnest application

1746. A meeting of the citizens was called on the ninth of February ; and Cap-tain Ebenezer Eastman and Mr. Henry Lovejoy were appointed a committee to " represent the difficult circumstances of the inhabitants of Rumford to the great and general court at Portsmouth, respecting the danger we are exposed to both from the French and Indian enemy, and request of them such aid and protection as they in their great wisdom shall think meet."

* See Appendix No. III.

to the Governor for military aid—and fortunately
Capt. Daniel Ladd, with a company of forty men
from Exeter, arrived in town the same day. There
had previously been a company stationed here from
Billerica, for a short time, and also one from Andover. The inhabitants were aware that a considerable body of Indians was in the vicinity, but had as
yet discovered but few, who were out on scouts.
The Indians themselves, hearing of Capt. Ladd's
approach, determined to lie concealed until Sunday
following, when they intended to massacre the people assembled in the meeting-house. But the people on Sunday went armed to their devotions, and
placed sentinels in different quarters to look out
for the approach of the Indians, who had the
night previous secreted themselves in the bushes
adjacent to the meeting-house, which stood nearly
on the spot now occupied by the dwelling of Mr.
John West. One party of them was concealed in
a thicket of alders,then growing where Dr. Green's
house now stands, and another was hid in the bushes on the north, between the meeting-house and
Mr. Emery's, near the prison. Some few of them
were seen by a little girl during the exercises, but
she did not make known the discovery until the
meeting closed, when the people marched out in a
body; and the Indians observing their arms, concluded to abandon the attack. They then retired

1747. *April* 2. Capt. Eastman. from Penacook, came into the house, and moved that the house would consider their circumstances at Penacook, with regard to
the enemy, and would grant them men to help them.—*Assembly Records.*

—— *April* 3. *Voted,* that there be allowed to John Osgood 12s. 6d. for expense
for coffins, &c. for the men killed at Rumford last year.—*Ibid.*

—— *Voted,* that his Excellency the Capt. General be desired to give orders for
enlisting or impressing 144 good effective men, to be employed under proper officers in defending the frontiers, guarding the people at work, and scouting, to be
posted as follows, viz. 30 at Rochester, 6 at Barrington, 10 at Nottingham, 20 at
Canterbury, 20 at Contoocook, 24 at *Penacook, &c.*— *Ib.*

—— *Nov.* 12. Phineas Stevens, Ebenezer Eastman and Jeremiah Clough, in behalf of the inhabitants of Contoocook, Rumford and Canterbury, petitioned for
aid against expected attacks from the Indians. *Nov.* 13. orders were issued for
enlisting 16 soldiers, five for each of said places.— *Ib.*

to the woods on the west towards Hopkinton, with the design to intercept Capt. Ladd and his men, who they supposed were to pass that way on the following morning.

On Monday morning, the 11th, seven of the inhabitants sat out for Hopkinton, two on horses, and the others on foot, all armed. They marched on leisurely, and *Obadiah Peters*, having proceeded some distance forward of the others into a hollow, about one mile and a half from the street, sat down his gun and waited the approach of his friends. The Indians, thinking themselves discovered, rose from their hiding-places, fired and killed Peters on the spot. At this moment, *Jonathan Bradley* and the rest of his party had gained the summit of the hill. Bradley was deceived in the number of the enemy, supposing the few whom he saw near Peters to compose the whole party. He ordered his men to fire, and they rushed down among them. The whole body of Indians instantly arose, being about 100 in number. Bradley now urged his men to fly for safety; but it was too late—the work of destruction had commenced. *Samuel Bradley* was shot through the body—stripped of his clothing and scalped. To Jonathan, they offered " good quarter," having been acquainted with him; but he refused their protection, his heroic spirit thirsting to avenge the death of his comrades. He fought with his gun against the cloud of enemies, until they struck him on his face repeatedly with their knives and tomahawks, and literally hewed him down. They then pierced his body, took off his scalp and clothes. Two others, *John Bean* and *John Lufkin*, attempting to fly, were killed by the same fire with Samuel Bradley. *Alexander Roberts* and *William Stickney* fortunately escaped death, but were made prisoners and taken to Canada. Immediately after the melancholy affair took place, an alarm was given from Walker's garrison to the people on the interval, and elsewhere, at

some little distance. They soon assembled and
consulted on measures of safety. The soldiers stationed at the garrison, and several of the inhabitants then repaired to the scene of slaughter. As
they approached, the Indians were seen upon the
retreat. The bodies were brought away in a cart,
and were interred in the church-yard on the following day.* The number killed of the Indians was
unknown to the inhabitants until some time after,
when the information was obtained from *Roberts*,
who had made his escape from captivity. He stated that four were killed, and several wounded, two
mortally, who were conveyed away upon litters,
and soon after died. Two they buried under a large
hemlock tree in the Great Swamp, about half a mile
south of the scene of slaughter. The other two
were buried at some distance from them, near Turkey river. Roberts found the two bodies under
the log after his return from captivity. The head
of one was taken away, it was supposed by wild
beasts. For the skull of the other, a bounty was
paid by the government.

Stickney, after about one year's detention in Canada, found means to escape with a friendly Indian,
and proceeded on his way home to within about one
day's journey of the white settlements, when they
fell short of provisions. The Indian directed Stickney to light a fire and encamp, while he would go
in quest of game. After Stickney had prepared
his camp, he went out to hunt, and in attempting to
cross a river on a log, fell in and was drowned.†

Jonathan Bradley was an officer in Capt. Ladd's
company, from Exeter, and stationed here for the
defence of the inhabitants. He was about thirty
years of age when killed ; and was the elder broth-

* Mr. Reuben Abbot, lately deceased at the age of 100 years, was fixed upon by
the inhabitants to bring away the bodies of his slaughtered townsmen. He procured an ox-cart at Eastman's fort, and brought away their bodies under the guard
of the soldiers and inhabitants. The writer was indebted to this venerable old
man for the particulars of the massacre.

† Tradition.

er of Samuel Bradley. He was a man of much coolness and decision; and his vigorous defence against the overwhelming force which crushed him to the earth, is sufficient proof of his determined bravery.

Samuel Bradley was a citizen of this town, and the father of the Hon. John Bradley, who died in 1815. He was a most amiable and promising young man; and his wife, who afterwards married with Richard Calfe, of Chester, and survived both, in the latter years of her life, used to speak with great affection of the husband of her youth, and of his tragical end. She died Aug. 10, 1817, aged 98 years.

Obadiah Peters, of Rumford, was probably a son of Seaborn Peters, who lived in J. Eastman's fort. It appears that at the time of his death he belonged to a company under the command of Capt. Nathaniel Abbot. He had been out in the expedition against Cape Breton, in 1745, in the company commanded by Capt. Eastman.

John Bean was from Brentwood, and *Lufkin* from Kingston.

The initials of those who fell were soon after marked on a large tree, standing near the fatal spot, which stood the only monument of the sanguinary conflict, until within a few years, some person cut it down. It is, however, pleasing to learn that the descendants of Samuel Bradley are about to erect a durable monument over the spot where their worthy ancestor was killed.

The Indians continued in the neighborhood, in small parties, and on the 10th of November following, killed a *Mr. Estabrooks*, on the road between the street and the place of the former massacre.

Early in February, 1747, the inhabitants empowered John Webster to apply to the General Assembly for military assistance. In his petition, he states that there were upwards of eighty families then residing in Rumford, and that they raised annually four times as much provision as was requisite for their own support. Having some reason to apprehend an attack from the Indians in considerable force, a petition was preferred to the Governor in June, stating that traces of the enemy had been discovered by the scouts ; that guns had been heard at Rumford and Contoocook at different times ; that from the situation of the inhabitants they were exposed to attacks from the enemy, the experience of the whole war having taught them, "that whenever any smart attack was made upon the settlements on Connecticut river, the enemy had never failed of sending a considerable number to visit their river," the Merrimack. The inhabitants at some seasons could work together in bodies, so as not to be so greatly exposed, but haying and harvesting now commencing, it was "impracticable without vast detriment to the whole, and utter ruin to some." A guard of twenty-four men was stationed here from the middle of March to the beginning of May ; and subsequently, by order of the Governor, thirty soldiers were detached for the assistance of the inhabitants, who remained with them until they had secured their crops.

October 23d, Dr. Ezra Carter, in behalf of the inhabitants of Rumford, represented by petition to the General Court, that they were "destitute of soldiers, and very much exposed both to the French and Indian enemy, and daily expect, by the experience of the last year, invasions by them, by reason of their killing one man on the 10th of November last, and on the 19th of said November, they were discovered by their tracks in a small snow, and pray your honors to consider our dangerous circumstances, and grant us such protection as you in your great wisdom shall think meet." In November, another guard of five men was ordered here, and similar assistance was afforded the inhabitants of Canterbury and Contoocook.

In the fall of 1747, a large party of Indians again made their appearance in the south-west part of the town, and for several weeks continued ranging about the woods, and destroying the cattle, horses, &c. of the inhabitants. Jeremiah Bradley had a fine field for fall grazing, and into this many of the citizens had turned their sheep and neat cattle. The reports from the guns of the Indians were frequently heard, and numbers of cattle were destroyed. The inhabitants at length rallied in a strong party armed, and proceeded cautiously in two divisions towards the enemy. In the woods near the field, one party found numerous packs, &c. belonging to the Indians, and concluded to await their approach in concealment. As they were approaching, one of the men, through accident, or an eager desire to revenge his losses, fired his musket, and alarmed the wary Indians, who, observing the smoke of the gun, filed off in an opposite direction. The whole party then fired, but with little injury to their tawny adversaries. The body of an Indian was, however, sometime afterwards found secreted in a hollow log, into which, it was supposed, having been wounded by the fire of the party, he had crawled, and expired.

In August of this year died Capt. EBENEZER EASTMAN, one of the wealthiest and most active of the early settlers. He was born at Haverhill, Ms. in 1689. His father's house and buildings were destroyed, with several others, by the Indians in their memorable attack upon Haverhill, March 15, 1698.* Young Eastman, at the age of 18, joined the regiment of Col. Wainwright in the expedition against Port Royal. In 1711, when the British fleet under Admiral Walker arrived in Boston harbor, the land forces were organizing with great despatch. Eastman now had the command of a company of sol-

---

* There is a tradition in the family, that sometime previous to this, Eastman's father and a Mr. Abbot, from Andover, were made captives by a party of the Penacook Indians, and were carried to what was afterwards called Sewall's island in the river in this town. No particulars can be collected.

diers, and embarked in one of the transports. The
fleet soon sailed up the St. Lawrence, and met with
no accident "until they got up off the *Virgin*
" *Mountains;* the weather then proving foggy,
" and the wind freshening, the Admiral asked the
" pilots what was best to do ? who advised that as
" the fleet was on the north shore, it would be best
" to bring to, with their heads to the southward."*
The Admiral obstinately refused : and the awful
consequence was the destruction of nine ships, the
loss of many lives, and the total failure of the expedition, which was designed for the conquest of
Canada. The part which Capt. Eastman acted on
this occasion, though noticed by none of the historians, is thus related by his grandson,† now living.
The pilots, who were perfectly aware of their peril, being well acquainted with the river, could not
but be panic-struck at the orders of the admiral,
which the captains of the transports seemed bent
to follow. Eastman, whose company was on board
one of them, represented to the captain their imminent peril, and beseeched him to " haul to wind-
ward, that they might escape the breakers." The
captain was a true *loyalist*, and exclaimed " he
would follow his commodore, if he went to h—ll."
Eastman then stated the circumstances to his men,
and informed them that if they would support him,
he would assume the control of the vessel, and attempt to shun the rocks. This he accordingly did,
by ordering the captain to his cabin, and the helms-
man to alter his course. They escaped wreck, and
when the following morning exhibited to the eyes
of the astonished crew, the bodies of the dead and
wrecks of the vessels which covered the St. Lawrence, the humbled captain, on his knees, acknowledged his deliverer, and desired his friendship. In
the morning, Capt. Eastman appeared before the
Admiral, who abruptly asked—" Capt. Eastman,

---

* Penhallow.
† Jonathan Eastman, Esq.

where were you, when the fleet was cast away?" "I was following my commodore," replied he. "Following your Commodore! (said the Admiral in surprise.) . . . . You d——d Yankees, are a pack of praying devils; you have saved your own lives, and prayed my men all to h——ll." Capt. Eastman soon after his return entered with zeal into the subject of a new settlement at Penacook. And during his life, was a persevering, influential and useful citizen. He was at the reduction of Louisbourg in 1745, and held a commission in the New-Hampshire forces, under the intrepid Vaughan. He died soon after his return, in his house on the east side of the river, which was then fortified against the attacks of the Indians.

From this period, it is not known that any serious mischiefs were committed by the Indians against the inhabitants of Rumford, although they occasionally suffered some losses in cattle and other property, which the savages chanced to meet with, while ranging through the woods and about the farms of the settlers. They were indeed in constant alarm, and for several years continued their addresses to government for the means of defence. The petition of Dr. Ezra Carter and another, in 1756, states, that "they had been subjected to great loss of time, for several years past by disturbances from the Indians, and particularly for the two last years past, about one fourth of the inhabitants had been driven from their settlements during the busy season of the year, and the whole obliged to divert their attention from husbandry to repair their garrisons, and provide for the safety of their families."

1748. Capt. John Chandler was elected representative of the town of Rumford to the General Assembly, on the 2d January. In March, the lines of the town were perambulated and marked.

In January, 1749, Benjamin Rolfe, in behalf of the inhabitants of Rumford, preferred a petition to the Governor and Council for an act of incorporation.* The proprietors of Bow remonstrated against the measure, and their influence prevailed.

A petition for the same purpose was also presented July 14th, 1756, by Ezra Carter, in behalf of the citizens. An act was framed, and after being read in the house of Assembly, was, through the influence of members interested in the Bow lands, rejected.

On the 28th of April, 1752, *Amos Eastman* of this town, in company with *John* and *William Stark* of Dunbarton, and *David Stinson* of Londonderry, being on a hunting expedition near Baker's river in Rumney, were surprized by a party of Indians, ten in number, of the St. Francis tribe. Eastman and John Stark were made prisoners; Stinson and William Stark, attempting to escape, were fired upon. Stinson fell, was dispatched, scalped, and stripped of his wearing apparel. His comrade succeeded in escaping. John Stark and Eastman were carried prisoners to Canada, and sold to the French. They remained in captivity about three months, were redeemed, and returned home. The Indians now exhibited signs of hostility at Canterbury. Rev. Mr. Walker went up to confer with them, and a chief returned with him to Rumford.† A short time after, two persons were taken away from Canterbury by the Indians.

---

* See Appendix, No. IV.

† Rev. Mr. Walker, who was beloved by all his parishioners, was also esteemed by the Indians, and when not in open war, they used to visit his house, where they were always well treated. At one time, they came to his house, complaining in angry terms that the white people possessed their lands unjustly. Mr. W. informed them that they were purchased of their chiefs, and that the deed, signed by them, was to be seen in Boston. He finally advised them to go and see it. To this they assented; and on their return, called and took some refreshments, and said that they had seen the paper, and were perfectly satisfied. This deed is the famous instrument of Wheelwright, now generally believed to be a forgery. After the peace, a number of warriors encamped near the minister's house. Mr. W. was absent, and his wife was under great apprehensions of injury. The Indians perceived this, and said to each other, "*minister's wife afraid.*" Upon this, one delivered her all the guns, and said they would call for them the next day. This they did, and were to her kind and affable.

From 1749 to 1766, the year after the incorporation of the town by the name of *Concord*, there are no records of the proceedings of the town or its officers. The town, in fact, existed only as a *parish of Bow*. About this time commenced the perplexing controversy between the proprietors of Bow and the inhabitants of Rumford. It is perhaps well known, that by the construction of the charter of Massachusetts, by King Charles II. in 1677, the jurisdiction of that state extended for three miles to the north of Merrimack river. The government of Massachusetts, in 1725, granted to sundry petitioners the township, afterwards called Rumford; and in 1728, made the grant of Suncook, now Pembroke, to the forty-seven soldiers, or their legal representatives, who were engaged with the celebrated Lovewell against the Indians at Pequackett. These two grants comprised about thirteen square miles, all lying within the supposed limits of Massachusetts. At the time of surveying and laying out the lands at Penacook, it appears that a committee was empowered by the government of New-Hampshire, to proceed to Penacook, and request the surveyors to desist from laying out the lands, as they were claimed by that government. They, however, proceeded to execute the business of their commission, and the plantation settled with much rapidity. In May, 1727, two years after the grant by Massachusetts, the government of New-Hampshire granted to Jonathan Wiggins and others, a tract of eighty-one square miles, which included more than two thirds of both Rumford and Suncook. No settlements were made, however, by the proprietors of Bow, nor did any difficulties arise in consequence of the conflicting grants, for about twenty years, during which time Rumford and Suncook had each settled a minister of the gospel, and converted the wilderness into fruitful fields.

Meantime the controversy between this state and
Massachusetts, respecting the boundary line, had
been carried before the King, and upon report of
commissioners appointed to mark out the dividing
line, he decided in 1740, that the northern boundary of Massachusetts should be a curve line pursuing the course of the Merrimack river, at three
miles distance on the north, beginning on the Atlantic ocean, and ending at a point due north of
Pawtucket falls; thence due west to his Majesty's
other possessions. By this determination, all the
settlements on the river above Pawtucket falls, fell
under the jurisdiction of New-Hampshire. There
was an express declaration, however, in the decision of the King, that *private property* should be
respected. The inhabitants of Rumford, immediately after learning the determination of the King,
petitioned to be restored to the province of Massachusetts; but were unsuccessful. In 1750, the
proprietors of Bow commenced numerous suits for
the ejectment of the settlers living within the limits of their grant. The course which they pursued
was extremely vexatious and calculated to prolong
the dispute, if not utterly to ruin many of the settlers, who had made great and expensive improvements on the lands. Every action was commenced
for so small a parcel of land, that, by a law of the
province, there could be no appeal home.*—The
courts and juries were interested in the lands, or
prejudiced against the settlers; and justice could
hardly be expected to result under such circumstances. The actions were continued to successive

* "But your petitioners' greatest misfortune is, that they cannot have a fair, impartial trial, for that the Governor and most of the Council are proprietors of Bow,
and by them not only the judges are appointed, but also the officers that impannel
the jurors; and the people are also generally disaffected to your petitioners on account of their deriving their title from the Massachusetts. And all the actions that
have hitherto been brought are of so small value, and, as your petitioners apprehend, designedly so, that by a law of the province there can be no appeal from the
judgments of the courts to your Majesty in Council; and if it were otherwise, the
charges that would attend such appeals would be greater than the value of the
land, or than the party defending his title would be able to pay."—*Petition of Rev.
Mr. Walker and Benjamin Rolfe, Esq. to the King.*

terms, but decided by both inferior and superior Courts in favour of the plaintiffs. The defendants, and also the inhabitants generally of both Rumford and Suncook, now petitioned to the King for an impartial trial, and commissioned Rev. Mr. WALKER to proceed to England and lay all the circumstances before his Majesty, empowering him to defend the suits at the Court of St. James.

In 1753, upon the petition of the inhabitants of Rumford, the General Court of Massachusetts granted £100 sterling, towards the expense of defending the suits brought against them by the proprietors of Bow. The Massachusetts agent, Mr. Bollan, was instructed to use his endeavors to obtain such determination of his Majesty in Council, as should quiet the grantees of lands from that province in their possessions. Mr. Walker went to England in 1753, and again a short time after, and succeeded in obtaining a trial on appeal before a committee of the Lords of the Council. Sir William Murray, afterwards Lord Chief-Justice Mansfield, was his counsellor and advocate, with whom he formed a particular acquaintance. After a patient hearing of all the parties concerned, the committee of the Council reported, that the judgments of the courts of New-Hampshire in the case should be reversed, and the appellants be restored to " what they had lost by means of said judgments." This was approved by his Majesty in Council on the 29th December, 1762.*

Thus ended the disagreeable controversy with the proprietors of Bow, during the continuance of which, the inhabitants of Rumford had been without town privileges or government, and were harrassed with numerous vexatious suits, and subjected to the expense of attending almost every term of the courts, then exclusively holden at Portsmouth.

* See Appendix, No. V.

On the 17th June, 1765, the government of this
State granted the charter of the town of CONCORD,
comprising " a part of the town of Bow, and some
lands adjoining thereto." The bounds, as described in the charter, began " at the mouth of Contoocook river, which is the S. E. corner of Boscawen;
tl ence S. 73° W. by said Boscawen 4 miles ; thence
S. 17° E. 7 miles 100 rods; thence N. 73° E. 4
miles to Merrimack river, there crossing the river
and still continuing the same course to Soucook
river; then beginning again at the mouth of Contoocook river aforesaid, from thence running N. 73°
E. 606 rods from the easterly bank of Merrimack
river, or till it shall come to the S. W. line of
Canterbury ; thence S. E. on said line 2 miles 80
rods ; thence S. 17 E. to Soucook river aforesaid ;
thence down said river, till it comes to where the
line from Merrimack river strikes the Soucook river."

By the provisions of the act, the first meeting
was to be holden on the 3d Tuesday of August,
1765, and Samuel Emerson, Esq. was authorized to
call the first town meeting; but in consequence of
his neglect, no meeting was notified; and a special
resolve was passed by the Legislature on the 27th
November, of the same year, for calling a meeting
for the choice of town officers, &c. on the third
Tuesday of January, 1766.

1766.—At the first legal meeting of the inhabitants of *Concord*, Lt. Richard Hazeltine, who died
in 1818, was moderator; Peter Coffin was appointed clerk, and Joseph Farnum, Lot Colby and John
Chandler, jun. selectmen. The meeting for the
choice of officers for the year ensuing was holden
March 4th. On the 25th, another town meeting
was holden, and measures taken to provide schools
in the different sections of the town—there having
previously been but one school in town. Every
man was taxed " five days' work on the highways
and pound this year."

Dr. EZRA CARTER died Sept. 17, 1767, at the age
of 48. He was a native of South-Hampton, in this
state ; studied physic with Dr. Ordway of Salisbury, Mass. and settled in this place about 1740. He
was a good scholar, though not liberally educated
—a skilful practitioner, and a man universally beloved. Soon after his removal here, he was honored by the inhabitants with civil trusts, which he
executed with zealous fidelity. It is to be regretted that of Dr. Carter, as well as of others who
lived at a later day, so few particulars can be collected. Enough, however, is known to warrant the
assertion that few men excelled him in a benevo-
lent spirit and good humored exertions to promote
the peace and welfare of society. He was a man
of wit and pleasantry, and when called to visit the
sick and desponding, never failed to administer,with
his remedies for the body, a cordial to the mind.
Dr. Carter, though frequently menaced by the Indians, never suffered from their attacks. About
the time of the Bradley massacre, he had gathered
into winrows his hay then cut, on the plat of
ground extending on the west of the street, near
the site of the Capitol. During the night, several
Indians secreted themselves in the hay, intending
to surprise the Doctor on the following morning.
Providentially, a storm of rain commenced early in
the morning and continued for several days with
little abatement, during which the Indians retired.
After peace was restored, the Indians informed the
doctor of their meditated attack, and that conceiving the Great Spirit to have sent the rain for his
shelter, they dared not remain. On the 10th of
November, of the same year, (1746) a Mr. Estabrooks came for the doctor to visit a patient.
Through some difficulty in catching his horse, the
doctor did not immediately follow Estabrooks. In
a very short time, the alarm was given that Estabrooks was killed, and a party proceeding on the
road after him, found his body near the path. This

was one of the last acts of Indian hostility in this
section of the country.   On a certain occasion, Dr.
Carter was called to visit a sick family in Bow.   Added to their other sorrows, poverty had thrown around
them her tatters and rags.   Disease is ever loth to
quit such company.   The family were a long time
sick—the doctor was their constant attendant—and
on their recovery, the poor man felt new troubles
coming upon him.   "How, doctor," said the unhappy man, " am I to pay you, for all your kindness, your attention and medicine ? You see here a
large family, destitute of every thing, save the bare
necessaries of life."   " I have been faithful to you,"
replied the doctor, " and am I not entitled to a re-
ward ?" " You are, doctor, oh, you are !" said the
trembling wife, " but do wait a little—we can't pay
you now."   " I can inform you, my good friends,"
said the inexorable physician, " that I am *knowing*
to your having property enough to satisfy my de-
mands—and moreover, that I shall *have it* before
leaving the house." The poor family were thunder-
struck—they knew that no friendly feelings subsist-
ed between the proprietors of Rumford and Bow—
but had always heard the doctor applauded as a
man of benevolence and mercy. They knew not
what to do.   At this moment, away scampered a
flock of kittens across the room, which the doctor
seeing, caught one of them and put it in his pocket.
" I told you I should have my pay, (said the doctor)
—I have got it.—Good bye, and God bless you !"
Many anecdotes of this kind are related of him ;
and one of the last acts of his life, was equally no-
ble.   Just before his decease, he looked over his
accounts, filled out receipts against all poor persons, who were indebted to him, with directions
that his executors should deliver them to those concerned immediately after his death.   This was accordingly done.

1771.—On the 20th December, died BENJAMIN
ROLFE, Esq. who was one of the early settlers, a man

of talents and education, and for many years one of the principal citizens. He was for some time the only magistrate in town, and in all its public transactions, we find him conspicuous. Associated with the Rev. Mr. Walker, whose eldest daughter he married, he assisted in managing the defence of the inhabitants against the vexatious proceedings of the proprietors of Bow. And in the various papers drawn up by him, and other memorials he has left, are to be seen evidences of his care and ability. His widow subsequently married Benjamin Thompson, a school-master of this place, from Woburn, who was afterwards distinguished as Count Rumford. Lady Sarah Thompson died in Concord in 1792. Of her last husband, a more particular notice will be given hereafter.

1772.—At the annual meeting, £60 were " raised for making and repairing highways." Hitherto no specific sum had been appropriated, but the inhabitants devoted each year a certain number of days to that purpose. *April* 7, the parish voted to give $500 for the meeting-house, then the property of individuals; and raised $50 in addition, " to be given the proprietors of the meeting-house, in order to complete the bargain." Messrs. John Kimball, Thomas Stickney and John Bradley were authorized to provide materials and superintend the repairs of the house.

1773.—At the annual March meeting, A. M'Millen, Esq. was authorized to present a petition to the General Court, requesting " that the parish of Concord may be annexed to the county of Hillsborough, provided that there might be an inferior and superior court held annually in said parish."

1772. A meeting was holden the 7th of December this year, and Andrew M'- Millen, Esq. empowered " to petition the Hon. Gen. Court of the province (in behalf of the town) for the privilege of laying out roads, as other towns have, and also that the boundaries of *Concord* might be as extensive as the township of *Rumford* formerly was."

1774.—The General Court of Massachusetts, in consideration of the difficulties and embarrassments which the grantees of Rumford had sustained from the suits of the proprietors of Bow, granted them a township in Maine, which was also called Rumford, and was settled by inhabitants from this town.

1775.—The commencement of this year was a period of deep anxiety and gloom. The repeated acts of aggression, on the part of the mother country, had driven the colonies into measures of resistance, bold and decisive. The people were almost universally inspired with the belief that a struggle must ensue, and the lovers of freedom were every where " sounding notes of preparation." Every village, however remote from the probable scene of action, was filled with alarm, and groups of citizens were seen in almost every corner, debating the cause of their country. The alarm of the battle at Lexington spread with rapidity throughout the country. Immediately on the reception of the news here, a company of 30 men, under the command of Capt. Chandler, volunteered and repaired to Cambridge, where they remained a fortnight. Captains Abbot and Hutchins had now recruited companies for eight months' service and joined the American forces. They were in the engagement at Bunker's Hill. One person, *William Mitchell*, from this town, was killed; and a young man of the name of *Peter Kimball*, wounded.

A committee of the provincial congress, which met at Exeter in January, of this year, were directed to address circulars to the several towns, to call another convention. The selectmen called a meeting of the inhabitants of Concord on the 11th of

1773. Lt. John Chandler was the first grand juror called from Concord, appointed Feb. 22, 1773.

1774. At the March meeting, Peter Green, Esq. was directed to present a petition to the General Court for leave to send a representative.

May, and Timothy Walker, jun. was elected " to represent the inhabitants of Concord at the General Convention of Deputies, from the several towns in this government, to be held at Exeter, the 17th of May," and fully empowered " to pursue such measures as may be judged most expedient to restore the rights of the colonies"—to serve for six months. At the expiration of this period, he was again elected to serve for a year. The town at their meeting in December, " voted to pay Capt. Abiel Chandler and others, who went to Cambridge upon the alarm in April, at the same rates allowed other troops of the colony."

There remained in almost every town some staunch friends of the government, who, viewing the attempt of the colonies to shake off their allegiance as desperate and hopeless, preferred either to retire within the acknowledged protection of the King's troops, or to remain inactive and neutral. Benjamin Thompson had already adopted the former course ; and there were several others who remained in town. But neutrality is esteemed little better than *treason* in times like these. And to the moral habits of the people, much more than to their feelings, wounded as they were by any apparent treachery or neglect of duty, were the opposers of the great cause indebted for their personal safety.

1776.—Committees of safety were now appointed in the several towns of the colony, whose instructions were derived from the general committee appointed by the provincial Congress. Their powers were extensive ; the trust one of great responsibility—and none but the firmest whigs were appointed. Messrs. *Philip Eastman, Thomas Stickney, Timothy Walker, jun. Joseph Hall, jun.* and *Richard Herbert*, were appointed the committee of safety in Concord for this year.

1777.—Measures were this year taken for the remuneration of soldiers engaged in the service of

the country from this town ; and £460 were raised
for the purpose. The sum of £100 was also appropriated for the use of the town, in the purchase
of ammunition, &c. This year, several individuals,
suspected of disaffection to the great cause of the
country, were arrested, and conveyed to Exeter, by
a number of the citizens of this place. A short
imprisonment, or the public denunciation of the
people in town meeting, who declared them to be
" enemies to their suffering country, and unworthy
the countenance of its friends"—had the effect to
subdue their loyal spirit; and when the almost
certain prospect of success filled the hearts of the
patriotic multitude with joy and gratitude, they too,
could join in the general triumph.

1778.—At a town meeting in January, Col. *Thomas Stickney* was instructed " to use his influence
at the next session of the General Assembly, that
a full and free representation of the people of this
state be called as soon as conveniently may be, for
the sole purpose of laying a permanent plan or sys-
tem for the future government of this state."

In 1779, a convention, called for that purpose,
drew up a Plan of Government, and sent it forth
among the people; but so deficient were its general provisions, that it was rejected.

Another convention was soon called, which had
nine sessions, and continued from June, 1781, to
Oct. 1783. Their first plan of government was

1777. *Committee of Safety.*—Messrs. John Kimball, Thomas Stickney, Reuben
Kimball, Benjamin Emery and Richard Herbert.

1778 Col. Timothy Walker was elected a member of the convention which
met at Concord this year. The convention met in the meeting house. Meshech
Weare was chairman. In December, Mr. Nathaniel Rolfe was chosen to represent the parish in the General Assembly to be holden at Exeter.

1779. The parish proposed to give up the pew ground to any number of persons
who would finish the meeting house, and add a porch ; and the value of another
porch ; and to be at the expence of building the steeple. July 19th, the town
voted to raise £1124 8 0, in addition to what had already been raised, for defraying
the parish expenses of that year. Sept. 6, the same year, the adjourned meeting
voted to raise £500 more. The question was taken on the acceptance of the plan
of government offered to the people, and there were 26 in favor, and 25 against

printed and sent to every town ; and the inhabitants were requested to state their objections to any particular part.

1782.—At the town meeting in Concord, Jan. 21st, " it was put to vote to see if the parish would accept the plan of government, as it now stands, and there appeared 48 against said plan, and none for it.

" *Voted*, to have a town representation.

" *Voted*, to have a Governor at the head of the legislative body.

" *Voted*, that the Governor shall not have a privy council.

" *Voted*, that the people at large shall appoint their militia officers."

A second plan was sent out by the convention assembled at Concord, which was most generally approved, but was not completed when the news of peace arrived.—The old form, having expired with the war, was revived for one year by the votes of the people in town-meetings.

A meeting of the inhabitants of Concord was holden Nov. 29th, for the purpose of considering the second plan of government, proposed by the convention. A committee, consisting of Col. Tim-

1780. *July.* The town at a full meeting, voted to give the soldiers that had lately " engaged to serve in the Continental Army, *ten bushels of corn* per month, or money equal thereto." In March, Col. Thomas Stickney was appointed agent to petition the General Assembly, for the extension of the limits of the town, to the ancient boundaries of Rumford. Major Jonathan Hale, in December, was instructed " to join in calling a convention to settle a plan of government for this State."

1781. In the beginning of this year, the General Court having called for sixteen soldiers, Capt. Aaron Kinsman, Lieut. Ezra Carter, Lieut. Asa Kimball, and Ensign James Mitchel, were appointed a committee to procure them. They were enlisted principally in this town. Feb. 6th, the town "voted to raise 1000 Spanish milled dollars, in order to enable the parish to procure the soldiers that are now called for to fill up the Continental army." The selectmen were authorized to lease all the interval lands, and the house lot belonging to the school right, for seven years. Timothy Walker was authorized to petition for a lottery, to build a bridge over Merrimack river; also to support the petition for extending the bounds of the town.

1782. At the annual meeting this year, the inhabitants voted $5 for every grown wolf, and $2,50 for every whelp ; 2s. per day were to be allowed for labor on highways.

othy Walker, Col. Thomas Stickney, Capt. Benjamin Emery, Capt. Reuben Kimball, Lt. John Bradley, Dr. Peter Green and Mr. Henry Martin, were
appointed to take the subject into consideration,
and report thereon. At the next meeting, Dec.
16th, there were 52 voters present, all of whom
" voted to reject the new constitution, in its present
form ;" but proposed the following amendments,
viz : " that the Governor and Privy Council be
left out, and that there be a President, a Legislative
Council, and a House of Representatives ; and that
the powers which are vested in the Governor and
Council be vested in the Council and House of Representatives." On the question of adopting the instrument, with those amendments, there were 30
votes in the affirmative.

On the 2d September, 1782, died the venerable
TIMOTHY WALKER, the first minister, and one of the
first settlers, of the town of Concord. He was
born at Woburn, Mass. in 1706; and after having
graduated at Harvard college, in 1725, he pursued
the usual course of theological studies. On the
18th of November, 1730, upon the unanimous invitation of the proprietors of the newly granted
township of Penacook, he was ordained their pastor.* After his ordination, Mr. W. returned with the
council, and soon came up with his wife, and other
settlers, with four of their wives. These were the
first women that came into the town, excepting two
who passed the previous winter in the block-house,
(meeting-house.) Mr. W. erected his house on *Horse-
shoe pond* hill; but after the Indians became hostile, he removed his house into a fort which he erected, and remained within its walls, with seven other
families, until the wars, in which the Indians engaged, were ended. During this time, the house
of worship stood without the walls of the garrison,

---

* See notice of Mr. Walker's settlement, p. 13.

where the inhabitants attended armed and in companies.

Many anecdotes are related of Mr. W. which prove him to have been a favorite with the Indians, who, even in times of danger and hostilities, were hospitably entertained within the walls of his fort. The merciless cruelties of the Indians, exercised most frequently upon the weak and defenceless, had created a sentiment of hostility against them, which now, as their extermination seemed rapidly approaching, rendered these little offices of friendship very delightful to them. An Indian never forgets a benefit, and many of them regarded Mr. W. as a father and friend.

The years of Mr. W. until the dispute between Bow, (or rather the government of New-Hampshire) and Concord, were passed in opening and improving his farm, and in the discharge of his parochial duties. At this time, he was chosen agent for the town to defend their law suits, and for this purpose made three voyages to England. Sir William Murray, afterwards Lord Mansfield, was his counsellor and advocate in the first cause. The last case detained him in England about two years. During this period, he had frequent interviews with Lord Mansfield at his Chambers, who the year before, was his counsel, and the conversation was often relative to the affairs of America. Mr. Kilby, an eminent merchant of Boston, was at that time in London, and introduced Mr. W. to many of the Ministry. From the manner and spirit of their remarks, when they spoke of America, he was convinced, and observed to the late Dr. Chauncey, " that nothing but the absolute submission of the colonies would satisfy Britain, and that, in the end, we must have a war with Old England and a league with France." He was ever a firm advocate for the rights of the colonies, and at the commencement of hostilities in 1775, although far advanced in years, he encouraged the people to be decided and persevering in their struggle for Independence. He was chosen by the town a delegate to the first Provincial Congress, and evinced great ardor in the American cause, and an unshaken conviction of its justice and success. He did not live, however, to see the truth of his predictions, and the accomplishment of his most sanguine wishes.

Mr. Walker's zeal in the cause of his country was firm and untiring. When Capt. Jonathan Eastman returned from Bennington, bringing the first intelligence of the victory, Mr. Walker came running out to meet him, eagerly inquiring " What news ? friend Eastman ! what news ?" The captain related to him the joyful tidings ; and the good old patriot exclaimed, " Blessed be God ! the country is saved—I can now die in peace !"

In his ministry, Mr. Walker was extremely tolerant. Firm in his own tenets ; yet to others of different persuasions, kind and charitable; forcibly recommending to all, what he adopted himself, the Bible alone as the rule of their faith and practice. Under his ministry, for 52 years, the town was harmoniously united in one congregation, and he died universally lamented by a people, among whom he had lived in honor and usefulness.

The constitution of 1783 was accepted by the people, and introduced at Concord, June 2d, 1784, by a religious solemnity.

Until this period, the town had been styled and recognized in all its proceedings, as " the *parish* of Concord," being thus named, in the act of incorporation. January 2d, this year, by an act of the legislature, " a gore of land lying at the north-east corner of Concord, consisting of about 1050 acres, in Loudon and Canterbury," was annexed to " the *town* of Concord."

1783. Labor on the highway, 4s. per diem. At a meeting Sept. 29, this year, " voted to receive the Constitution of Government as altered in June last." Yeas 20. Nays 10.

1785.—The main-street was laid out by a committee, consisting of Messrs. Benjamin Emery. Joseph Hall, John Bradley, Reuben Kimball and Joseph Farnum.

1786.—Though the State had now recovered from the anxieties and dangers of a revolution, a spirit of disquietude still existed among the people. The large debt occasioned by the war threw heavy burthens upon them, and the constant depreciation of the currency, aided by its frequent issue, caused loud complaints. The call for a new emission of paper was incessant and clamorous. In almost every town, meetings were holden and the subject debated with warmth. The citizens of Concord, however, in town meeting, voted, " that it was inexpedient for this state to make paper money on any plan whatever." Those who were zealous for paper currency, and against the laws which obliged them to pay their debts, now became clamorous against the courts and lawyers: they held them up as public nuisances, and wished to abolish the one, that they might impose a sufficient check upon the exactions of the other. An attempt was made to call a convention at Concord, during the session of the legislature, who should petition the government in favor of the plan. It was thought that the presence of a large body of men, convened under such circumstances, would have great weight. The attempt was defeated in a manner singular and ludicrous.

At the first sitting of the assembly in June, when only five members of the proposed convention were in town, some wags, among whom were several young lawyers, pretended to have been chosen by the towns in which they lived for the same purpose. In conference with the five, they penetrated their views, and persuaded them to post an advertisement, requesting all the members who were in town to assemble immediately, it being of the utmost im-

7

portance to present their petition as early in the session as possible. By this mean, sixteen pretended members, with five real ones, formed themselves into a convention, choosing one of the five their president, and one of the sixteen their clerk. They carried on their debates and passed votes with much apparent solemnity. Having framed a petition, complaining in the most extravagant terms of their grievances; praying for a loan of THREE MILLIONS of dollars, funded on real estate; for the abolition of inferior courts, *and a reduction of the number of lawyers to only two in each county;* and for a free trade with all the world; they went in procession to the Assembly, (some of whom had been previously let into the secret) and with great formality presented their petition, which was suffered to lie on the table. The convention then dissolved—the petition was withdrawn—and when others, who had been really chosen by the towns, arrived, they were exceedingly mortified on finding their views for that time so completely frustrated. The proceedings of this mock convention were, for a long time, subjects of sport and ridicule.

The public excitement, however, did not stop here. County conventions were called—petitions presented to the legislature—and the ferment at last subsided in the arrest and punishment of the rioters at Exeter.*

The meeting-house was this year finished, and the pews disposed of. At a meeting in December, the town voted "to give Mr. *Jonathan Wilkins* a call to the pastoral care of the church; and a salary (in case he accepted) of £100, with the use of the parsonage, excepting the meadow lot—beside £200 as a settlement." Mr. Wilkins did not accept the invitation.

At their annual meeting in 1788, the town voted to petition the legislature for a *new county.* Col. Timothy Walker was appointed agent, and directed

---

* See Belknap's account of the insurrection, &c. vol. ii. ch. 27, Hist. N. H.

to correspond with gentlemen in other towns upon the subject. *Sept.* 1, the inhabitants voted to give Mr. ISRAEL EVANS a call to the ministry, with £90 salary, and the use of the parsonage, three acres excepted, which had been disposed of; and also £15 addition to his salary annually, instead of a 'settlement.'

In March, 1789, Mr. Evans accepted the call of the church and people, and his installation took place on the 1st July following. Introductory prayer, by Rev. Jeremy Belknap; Discourse, by Rev. Mr. Eckley, of Boston; Ordaining prayer, by Rev. Mr. Woodman; Charge, by Rev. Dr. Macclintock; Fellowship of the Churches, by Rev. Mr. Colby; and Concluding prayer, by Rev. Mr. Smith.

Rev. Mr. Evans continued to preach unto the people of this place, until 1797. In April, of that year, he announced his " intention of resigning to the town their pulpit, and of finishing his work of the ministry in the place on the first of July." The town signified to him their approbation of his intention, and appointed a committee to wait upon the Ecclesiastical Council, and lay before them the proceedings of the town in that respect. The Council approved of their proceedings; and as no formal charges had been exhibited against Mr. Evans, they recommended him " to the churches, and to the work of the ministry, wherever God in his providence might open a door."

Measures were taken without delay to settle another clergyman, and on the 28th December, the town voted to invite Mr. ASA M'FARLAND to settle among them. A salary of $350, with the use of all the improved lands of the parsonage, was voted, with " liberty to cut what wood and timber on the out-lands he might need." Jan. 27, 1798, Rev. Mr. M'Farland, in an affectionate letter to the church and people, accepted their call to the pastoral care of the church; and his ordination took place on the 7th March following. The officiating clergy-

men, were the Rev. Stephen Peabody, of Atkinson ;
Rev. John Smith, of Hanover ; Rev. Joseph Woodman, of Sanbornton ; Rev. Zaccheus Colby, of
Pembroke ; Rev. Frederick Parker, of Canterbury ;
Rev. Jedidiah Tucker, of Loudon ; and Rev. Jo-
siah Carpenter, of Chichester. Mr. M'Farland was
a native of Worcester, Mass., born April 19, 1769 ;
was graduated at Dartmouth College in 1793, and
afterwards served as a tutor for two years. The
degree of D. D. was conferred upon him by Yale
College, under the venerable Dwight, in 1809, and
the same year, he was appointed a trustee of Dartmouth College. This latter appointment, he resigned in 1821.*

On the 21st June, 1798, died Major DANIEL LIVER-
MORE, aged 49. He was an active officer during the
revolution, and in many of those important battles
which decided the fate of the contest. He was a
useful citizen, and was repeatedly honored by his
fellow townsmen.

With the public transactions of the town subse-
quent to this period, perhaps every citizen is well
acquainted. Its proceedings have been those
merely which related to its internal affairs, and are
too recent, too fresh in the memory, to need recital.
It is interesting, however, to glance at the rapid
improvements in business and wealth which have
been made here within the last twenty years. In
1798, there were but two or three trading houses in
town ; the settlements were thinly scattered ; and
though there were then several enterprising and active citizens, engaged in business, the village did
not exhibit that outward show of prosperity
which it does at present. The grounds where the

---

* The ancestors of Dr. M'Farland were among that colony of Scots, who, in
the reign of James I., removed to the province of Ulster, in Ireland. His grand-
father, Andrew M'Farland, emigrated to this country, and settled in Worcester,
about the time of the settlement of Londonderry, in this State. He left three sons,
William, James and Daniel. William died at Worcester, and also James, the
father of Dr. M'F.—Daniel removed to the western part of Pennsylvania, about
the commencement of the revolution, and finally settled on the Monongahela,
where his descendants now live.

lofty edifices erected by the State are situated, were then covered with bushes and trees; and if the prophecy of a facetious legislator, who dreaded some Egyptian visiters, had no foundation, he might have stated that its thickets *had* afforded shelter to far less musical animals.

The public buildings are the Capitol, the State Penitentiary, the Court-House, and the meeting-house.

The building of the Capitol was commenced in 1816; and the legislature convened in its halls in 1819. It is situated in the centre of the village, upon a gently inclined plane between Main and State streets, and has two regular fronts, east and west. The centre of the building is fifty feet in front by fifty-seven in depth; the wings are each thirty-eight feet in front by forty-nine in depth; the whole making a parallelogram of one hundred and twenty-six feet in length by forty-nine in width, with the addition of a projection in the centre of each front of four feet. It is two stories above the basement, which rises five feet above the surface of the ground: the first story is nineteen feet; the second eighteen feet in the wing, and thirty-

1790. *Aug.* 30. The town voted "one hundred pounds for building a house for the accommodation of the General Court," to be 80 by 40 feet, and 15 feet post.

1792. *Oct.* 11. The 11th regiment, for the *first* time paraded on Eastman's plain.

1794. *Dec.* 8th, The town voted "to give, in addition to the Continental pay for the town's quota of minute-men, so much as shall make each one's pay eight dollars per month, and one month's pay to be advanced to each man when they shall be called to march."

1796. The inhabitants voted to finish the town-house, and appropriated £60 for that purpose.

1797. At a meeting in December, it was "voted that the men that enlist, shall have ten dollars with what the Congress give, and if called into service to have one month's pay in advance." Also, "voted that the selectmen give those persons that shall enlist, a HANDSOME TREAT at the expense of the town."

1798. This year, the lines between Concord and Loudon, were perambulated and fixed by the selectmen of the respective towns.

1800. Lines between Hopkinton and Concord, and Canterbury and Concord, perambulated by the selectmen; and again in 1808.

1805. Lines run between Boscawen and Concord by selectmen.

1813. Bye-laws adopted relative to extinguishing of fires.

one in the centre. The roofs of the wings are lev-
elled at the outer ends and rise ten feet against the
body of the centre ; the roof of the centre rises
thirteen feet, presenting gable ends in front ; from
the middle of which, the cupola rises, eighteen
feet square, to the height of fifteen feet above the
ridge ; thence in an octangular form, thirteen feet
in diameter, seventeen feet, and is covered with a
roof in the form of an inverted acorn rising to the
height of nine feet, and surmounted with a gilt
ball, thirty-three inches in diameter, on which stands
an eagle six and a half feet in height, with its
wings partially expanded. Each front has in its
lower story three doors and six windows, and in its
upper story, nine windows, with a semi-elliptical
window in each gable end : four windows in the
south, and two in the north end. The outside walls
of the building are of granite stone, hammered, and
built in a plain style—the only ornament being a
Tuscan frontispiece of stone work at each central
front door. The roof and cupola are of wooden
materials. The roof is ornamented with a coving
appropriate to the Doric order, and a balustrade upon the wings. The square part of the cupola is
ornamented with twelve Ionic columns, three at
each corner, placed in a triangular position, with
an appropriate coving and balustrade. The octangular part has one Ionic column at each corner,
surmounted with an urn.

In the second story of the centre is the Representatives' chamber, with an arched ceiling rising
thirty feet from the floor, elegantly finished with
stucco-work. The north wing contains the Senate
chamber, eighteen feet in height, with a beautiful
ceiling of plaistering, ornamented with stucco-work,
supported by four Ionic columns and an equal
number of pilasters. This room, for its neatness
and elegance of finishing, is not perhaps inferior to
any in the United States. In the south wing are
contained the Council chamber and anti-chamber,

both of which are finished in a handsome style. In the same wing, in the lower story, which is divided into two parts, are the Secretary's and Treasurer's offices, over which is a suite of committee rooms. In the north wing, under the Senate chamber, is a spacious room intended for public hearings before committees of the legislature. Under the Representatives' chamber, is an open area, in which are eight Doric columns, supporting the flooring above. This area, with the adjacent passages in the wings, cooled by the current of fresh air passing through the spacious doors and windows opening into them, affords, in the warm month of June, a delightful retreat to legislators, when fatigued by long attention to their arduous duties, or heated by the ardor of debate, above stairs; and it is by no means an uncommon case to see them availing themselves of the benefits of this pleasant retirement.

The lot on which the State House stands contains something more than two acres, enclosed on its sides with a solid wall of hammered stone about five feet high; the front fences are of stone posts and sills and iron castings, with gates of the same material.

The expences of building this house, including the fences, the lot of ground on which it stands and the furniture of the house, amounted to nearly eighty-two thousand dollars. Few public buildings in the United States are superior to this in the beauty of its construction, or the convenience of its apartments. The architects were Messrs. Stuart J. Park and Levi Brigham; the superintending committee, Messrs. Albe Cady, William Low and Jeremiah Pecker. The lot of land on which the building stands, the stone for the house, and drawing the same, were furnished the State by a few public spirited individuals, at an expense of about $4000.

The State Prison was erected in 1812; and cost, with the appurtenances, about $37,000:

since which time nearly $5000 have been drawn
from the public treasury to defray the expense of
additional buildings, and a new work house, the
first one having been destroyed by fire in 1819.
The prison is situated on State street, north of the
Capitol, and is three stories high, built entirely of
granite. It is 70 feet in length, 36 feet wide, the
walls of which are three feet in thickness. It contains in all 36 cells, the dimensions of which are 8
feet by 9, with the exception of six in the upper
story, for the accommodation of the sick, &c. which
are 10 by 17. The yard is enclosed by a faced
wall of 259 feet by 192, fourteen feet high, surmounted by a range of pickets ten feet in length.
Connected with the prison, is a house for the accommodation of the warden, his family, guards,
&c., built also of granite, four stories high, exclu-
sive of the basement, and is 49 feet by 22. The
officers, &c. of this institution are a warden, physician, chaplain, deputy-warden, four guards, two
overseers of the work-shops—the whole of whom
receive their pay directly from the proceeds of the
prison, with the exception of the warden, whose
salary, $800, is drawn from the treasury. The
Governor and Council, for the time being, constitute the board of directors, or visiters. The con-
victs are employed in stone-cutting, coopering,
smithing, shoe-making, weaving, and tailoring.

The meeting-house was erected in 1751. Previous to this, the inhabitants worshipped in the
building, erected in 1727, for the defence of the settlement. In 1802, an addition was made to the
front of the present house, consisting of a semi-
circle, projecting thirty feet, and divided into seven
angles, with a gallery. This alteration makes the
house one of the largest and most convenient in
the State.

The county Court-House was originally the town
house, and was altered and repaired during the year
1823, expressly for the purpose of accommodating

the courts, at the expense, partly of the town, and partly of individuals. It is one of the most commodious county buildings in the State.

The Society of Friends have a meeting-house, standing near the Congregational church. And the building of a new brick church for the Baptists was commenced in the fall of 1823, a few rods south of the Capitol.

An act of the Legislature, passed July 1, 1823, constituting the county of Merrimack, established this town as the seat of justice. This measure, so highly beneficial to the people of the new county, will also prove a source of additional business to he town.

During the brief period which has elapsed since the commencement of the present century, many estimable and useful men have departed. Nearly all the children and grand-children of the first settlers have left the stage ; and a new generation, actuated by different motives, enjoying superior advantages, are succeeding them, reaping the fruits of their toils, their enterprize and watchfulness. It is to be hoped they will imitate their virtues, their strict moral habits, and their persevering industry in the common pursuits of life.

Biographical Notices.

It will not be deemed impertinent, in closing these brief sketches, to notice some of the most distinguished citizens of this town, who have deceased. In doing this, the writer is actuated by no other motive than a wish to perpetuate their good fame, and with it, the salutary influence of their examples. The memory of great and good men, whatever may have been their sphere of action, exalted or humble, should be warmly cherished, if not for the delight with which we may contemplate their character, and the lessons we may draw therefrom,—at least for the rich impressions it may give the generations that are to come.

If many names of worth and usefulness are left unnoticed, the apology must be, not that the writer was unwilling to extend these notices, but that, after a long period of diligent research, he has been able to obtain no more.

Sir BENJAMIN THOMPSON.

BENJAMIN THOMPSON, though not a native of this town, spent several years of usefulness in the place. He was born at Woburn, Mass. March 26, 1753. His father died while he was very young, leaving him to the care of a guardian. He received a common school education, and was placed first with Dr. Hay, a physician of Woburn, where during the intervals of study, he amused himself in making surgical instruments, &c. which he finished in a handsome style. He was next placed as clerk in a store at Salem. His aversion to this business was soon manifested, and he was oftener found with a penknife, file and gimblet under the counter, than with his pen and books in the counting-room. He was fond of the study of chemistry, and enthusiastic in his devotion to mechanics and mathematics. At Salem, he undertook to prepare some fire works, or rockets. While pounding the ingredients, it was supposed a particle of sand, treacherously concealed in the mass, caused a scintillation, and the whole exploded in his face and bosom. The injury which he experienced was severe, and added to a temporary loss of sight, the skin of his face and bosom was taken away with the bandages. Such an apprentice, it might easily be perceived, would not answer the purposes of a merchant.

Young Thompson continued his studies and philosophical inquiries with diligence. Among other things, he attempted to solve that great desideratum—*perpetual motion.* After residing at Salem and Boston about two years, he returned to his mother in Woburn, his friends receiving him with unwelcome pity, impressed with a belief that he would never fix his mind upon any regular employment, by which he could gain a support.

Through the kindness of a friend, Thompson was admitted to the philosophical lectures commenced at Cambridge about the year 1769; this was a rich feast to him, and he zealously improved his opportunity, making rapid advances in his favorite studies. In 1772, he commenced schoolkeeping in Bradford, Mass. ; and soon after removed to this town. He taught school here with success ; and afterwards married Mrs. Sarah Rolfe, widow of B. Rolfe, Esq. and daughter of the first minister of Concord, by whom he had one daughter, lately living in France. Pleased with parade and the beau monde, and enjoying from the goodness of nature all the personal recommendations, which attract the admiration of the world, he never appeared at public entertainments, or in fashionable circles, without being respectfully noticed. In an excursion, which he made from Concord to Portsmouth, with his lady, to be present at a military review or some holiday, his genteel appearance and manly, impressive address attracted the observation of many, and among others he was particularly noticed by the governor, Wentworth, who invited him to his party, and never spoke of Mr. Thompson but with delight. The civil and friendly manner, in which he had thus been treated by the Governor, was not mere etiquette, as was sufficiently manifested a little time afterwards, by having the offer of a Major's commission. This mark of esteem and confidence was peculiarly gratifying to Mr. Thompson, as he possessed a genius and taste for military operations.

Mr. Thompson lived with his wife about two years; when the revolution commencing, and being a staunch friend of the government, he was obliged to quit his family and rural residence; and he retired within the lines of the British army. In October, 1775, he went to Rhode-Island; embarked for Boston harbor; and in January following, sailed for England. On arriving in London, he was introduced to Lord Germaine, (afterwards Lord Sackville) then presiding at the head of the American department, who conceived a warm friendship for him. In his office, he enjoyed an honorable post, until, nearly at the close of the contest, he was sent over to New-York; raised a regiment of dragoons; obtained the provincial rank of lieutenant colonel, and became entitled to half-pay, which he received till his death.

After his return to England, in 1784, the King conferred upon him the honor of knighthood. This event was a prelude to public honors elsewhere.— Sir Benjamin Thompson had become acquainted with the minister of one of the most respectable German princes. This, together with his growing greatness, induced his Serene Highness the Elector Palatine, reigning Duke of Bavaria, to invite him into his service, and honorable terms were proposed to him. He applied for, and obtained the King's permission to proceed to Munich. Here he soon obtained considerable influence in public affairs— was instrumental in the introduction of various reforms in the police—and enjoying the confidence and patronage of the Prince, he had an opportunity to reduce to practice his schemes of economy and public improvement. He was soon raised to the highest military rank, and created a Count of the Empire. The remembrance of his native land, and of his youthful enjoyments in this town, induced him to add to his title that of *Rumford.* Mendicity had become a public calamity in many of the German cities, and threatened the most alarming consequences. Conceiving the project of applying a remedy, and having taken the proper measures, Count Rumford, at a given day and hour, accompanied by several military officers, and a body of troops, issued orders for seizing all the beggars at Munich ; and being determined to obviate the possibility of disgrace, attached to such a measure, he began by arresting the first proper object with his own hands. No sooner had he done this, than the officers and men, without making any scruple or difficulty whatever, cleared the streets with promptness and success ; but at the same time with all imaginable good nature—so that in the course of a single day, not a beggar was to be seen in the whole range of the metropolis. But to sweep away the whole mendicant tribe, would have done nothing effectual, had not houses of industry been opened for their constant employment, and wholesome viands been procured them. His scheme succeeded admirably. By active exertions, he introduced various manufactures, and thus affording employment to the poorer classes, prevented a renewal of former scenes of indolence, suffering, and vice.— Wherever he went, his schemes for the public advantage were well received ; and his fame, as a philosopher and philanthropist continued to increase. He received many favors from the sovereigns of the continent. The Elector Palatine created him a Count, and procured for him the order of St. Stanislaus, from the King of Poland; made him a knight, chamberlain, privy counsellor of state, lieutenant general in his service, as Duke of Bavaria, colonel of his regiment of artillery, and commander-in-chief of the general staff of his army. He was also honored by all the learned societies of Europe, and of his native country. But these high-sounding titles were mere baubles, when compared to his just fame as a philosopher. He made liberal bequests to different institutions in his native country ; and died at his country seat of Auteuil, France,

where he had spent the latter years of his life, in
1814. An eloquent eulogy on his character was
read before the Institute of France, by M. Cuvier,
Jan. 9, 1815, in which a just view is taken of his
various discoveries in science, and of his personal
exertions and fame.

Little did his friends, who witnessed with sorrow
his juvenile pranks, his disregard of any regular
business, anticipate his future fame. Little did the
scholars who attended to his instructions in this
village in 1773–4, and who were sometimes amused
with his athletic exercises, and his odd experiments
—dream that their master was to be clothed with
the stars of princes, and acquire a fame that should
be lasting and honorable. While contemplating his
character, we do not stop to inquire the motives
which induced him to abandon the cause of his native country ; but reflect, that, though driven from
her shores, and grown illustrious amongst her enemies, he yet bequeathed to her institutions his estate, to her citizens his fame.

Hon. THOMAS W. THOMPSON.

On the first day of October, 1821, died the honorable THOMAS W. THOMPSON. He was born in
Boston, Mass. in the month of March, in the year
1765. His father, the late deacon Thomas Thompson, was a native of Alnwick, in North-Britain.
His mother, Isabella White, was born in Glasgow,
in Scotland. The period of their emigration from
Europe to Boston is not recollected. They removed from Boston to Newburyport, when he was
quite young. He was fitted for college at Dummer Academy, in the parish of Byfield, in Newbury, Mass. by the venerable Samuel Moody, a Pre-
ceptor, who was no less distinguished for talent at
governing his pupils, than for his thorough knowledge of the Latin, Greek, and Hebrew languages.
He entered the college at Cambridge in the year
1782, and received the degree of A. B. in 1786.

Soon after he left college, the insurrection in Massachusetts, of which Daniel Shays was nominal leader, broke out, and he entered into the army as an aid to General Lincoln, commander of the army of Massachusetts, and served during the whole campaign, in a severe winter, and until the insurrection was quelled. He afterwards pursued the study of Theology, in order to qualify himself for the pulpit. While engaged in that study, he was appointed a Tutor in the College at Cambridge ; he accepted the appointment, and was very much a favorite with the students, to whom he was rendered peculiarly agreeable by the suavity of his manners, and native, easy, unaffected politeness—qualities, at that day, too rare among the learned instructors of colleges. Leaving the office of tutor, he commenced the study of law, under the tuition of Theophilus Parsons, " the giant of the law," who then lived at Newburyport. Being admitted to practice at the bar, he came into New-Hampshire in June, 1791, and commenced practice near the south meeting-house, in Salisbury, where he remained about one year, and then removed to the river road, in Salisbury, where he continued in the practice of law until he went the first time to Washington, a representative in Congress. He then withdrew from judicial courts, though he continued through life to give advice as a counsellor at law. Soon after he came into this State, his talents, industry, integrity, and knowledge of the law, introduced him to a very extensive and lucrative practice, and he became well known at the bar, in most of the counties in this State.

In the year 1801, he became a member of the board of trustees of Dartmouth college, and continued such, until he resigned his seat a short time before his death. Of this board, he was an active and efficient member. He was, from 1805 to 1807, a Representative, and once a Senator in the Congress of the United States. He represented the

town of Salisbury once or twice in the Legislature.
After his removal to Concord, he was several times
elected a Representative of that town. He was
Speaker of the House of Representatives of this
State at a time when party spirit was at its greatest height ; and, even at that time, his political
opponents bore willing testimony to his candor,
ability and impartiality in the discharge of the duties of that office.

In the year 1809, he removed from Salisbury to
Concord, where he ever after resided until his
death. In August, 1819, he sat out on a journey
to Quebec, and was on board the steam-boat Phœ-
nix, bound from Burlington to Canada, at the time
of its destruction by fire at midnight on lake Cham-
plain. The vessel was all on fire, and the people
on board were leaving her in two small boats,
while he was left asleep. Waking, he saw the situation of the vessel, and that the last boat was
leaving her. He jumped into the boat, already filled
nearly to sinking, and was the last person who
escaped from the burning vessel. The terrors and
fatigue of that night probably produced the disease
which put a period to his life.

Hon. TIMOTHY WALKER.

The honorable TIMOTHY WALKER, son of the first
minister of Concord, was born in 1737, on the paternal farm where he died, May 5, 1822. His ear-
lier years were employed in the pursuits of husbandry, and the acquirement of an education ; he
was a good farmer, and his reputation as a scholar
stood high in the class which graduated at Cambridge in 1756. He at first designed to engage in
the work of the ministry, and qualified himself for
that purpose. But the increasing complaints of his
country were to him the premonitions of a mighty
struggle, and convinced him that she would soon
need active spirits on her side. He resolved to re-

linquish his favorite design, and exert himself for the good of his country.

At the commencement of the revolution, a period of much doubt and peril, when most men were agitated, and many trembled for the fate of the colonies—Walker was found among the most judicious, yet determined supporters of the revolution. In almost every town of the country there were many still loyal to the British crown, and who, though in common with their fellow citizens they felt its unhallowed oppressions, were yet willing to endure them. To counteract their exertions was required the utmost vigilance of every friend of liberty. At this critical moment, when the alternative presented of abandoning the country, or arresting her inbred enemies—when personal friendships must be sacrificed at the altar of freedom, and the charities of private life be broken off in watchfulness of public enemies,—Walker was eminently useful; and though he exerted himself to prevent unnecessary riots or tumultuous proceedings, he was vigilant in pursuing the proper course to subserve the interests of the country. He was entrusted with various duties by the government, and in 1776, was a member of the Committee of Safety for the State, who in the recess of Congress, exercised the powers of that body. He commanded a regiment of minute-men in New-Hampshire, was afterwards paymaster of the New-Hampshire forces, and served a campaign at Winter-Hill under General Sullivan. He was a member of the convention which formed our excellent Constitution, was afterwards frequently elected a Representative and Senator to the State Legislature, and was ever found an undeviating advocate of the cause of his country. He was for several years chief-justice of the court of common pleas, and was respected for his uprightness and candor.

9

At an advanced age, Judge Walker retired from active life to the enjoyment of his farm, and domestic ease and affluence. In private life, he was amiable and sincere ; in his manners, frank and honorable ; and in his conversation, exhibiting the agreeable powers of an independent and well cultivated mind. To the aged, he was a cheerful and kind companion ; to the young, a paternal friend and counsellor : and both had before them in his life a pattern of public and private rectitude.

Doctor PHILIP CARRIGAIN.

Doctor PHILIP CARRIGAIN, was born in the city of New-York, A. D. 1746. His father, who was also a physician, emigrated from one of the British ports, to that city ; where he died after a short residence. From the little that has been preserved of his history, it is known that he was for some time, a student, or an assistant, in one of the Hospitals in London ; and that he was in the service of the Pretender in Scotland, A. D. 1745 ; and from memorials he has left, appears to have been a finished scholar. Doct. C. was brought in his youth to Haverhill, Mass. where he studied physic with the late Doct. Bricket. He came to Concord in 1768, where he established himself as a physician and surgeon. There were then but few of the faculty, in this section of the country ; and as he discovered extraordinary skill and decision, in the management of the cases confided to him, he rose rapidly to the highest eminence in his profession, and for the greater part of his succeeding life, had a more extensive practice, than perhaps, any other physician of his time, in the State. He died in August, 1806. His lady died the December preceding. She was the daughter of the late Thomas Clough, Esq. of Canterbury, and was remarkable for the strength and fortitude of her mind ; and for her humanity and judgment, in attending and administering to the sick.

Rev. ISRAEL EVANS.

The reverend ISRAEL EVANS, the second clergy-man settled in Concord, was born in Pennsylvania in 1747 ; received his education at Princeton college, where he graduated in 1772 ; was settled here July 1, 1789 ; resigned his pastoral charge July 1, 1797. He was engaged previous to his settlement here, in the capacity of chaplain in the revolutionary army, and was the only chaplain, who continued in service during the whole struggle. He was with Montgomery before Quebeck—at the capture of Burgoyne—accompanied Gen. Sullivan on his Indian expedition, and witnessed the surrender of Cornwallis at Yorktown. His zeal in the cause of his country frequently led him to expose his life in battle ; particularly, in Sullivan's engagement with the Indians, where he acted as an aid to the general. He died on the 9th of March, 1807, at the age of 60 years.

Col. THOMAS STICKNEY.

Col. THOMAS STICKNEY died in this town on the 26th of January, 1809, in the 80th year of his age. He was a native of Bradford, Mass. and son of Lieut. Jeremiah Stickney, who settled in this town, when the former was but two years of age, about the year 1731. In common with others of his fellow-citizens, Stickney was exposed to the dangers of Indian warfare, and was useful to the settlement in forwarding active measures of defence. His brother, *William Stickney*, was taken by the Indians at the massacre of the Bradleys, in 1746, and was accidentally drowned on his return from captivity. Thomas, at the dawn of the revolution, was appointed to the command of a regiment of militia ; and besides several local military services, he was at the battle of Bennington, under the heroic Stark, and acquitted himself as a man of bravery.

Col. GORDON HUTCHINS.

GORDON HUTCHINS was a son of Ephraim Hutchins, and born at Exeter in 1733. At about the age of 13, he accompanied his father, who commanded a company in the expedition against Louisbourg, in the capacity of waiter ; but subsequently, held a lieutenancy in the army. Returning from the war, he married and settled in Harvard, Mass. ; from which place, in 1773, he removed to Concord. On hearing of the battle of Lexington, Lt. Hutchins repaired to Cambridge ; and soon afterwards, enlisted a company, which served an eight months' campaign. In 1777, on learning the perilous situation of the northern frontiers, Capt. Hutchins, who had again been at Cambridge, returning on a Sunday morning, entered the meeting-house ; addressed the minister, (Mr. Walker,) and after briefly stating the intelligence he had received respecting the situation of the northern armies, urged his fellow-citizens to volunteer in defence of their country. The appeal was seconded by their worthy and patriotic pastor, and a company of about thirty men was enrolled, and with them, he sat out on the following morning. Before their arrival at Bennington, Stark had immortalized himself, and averted the threatened danger ; but they had the satisfaction to witness the surrender of Burgoyne and his army at Saratoga. Previous to this, Capt. Hutchins had been at White-Plains, where he was promoted to the rank of lieutenant-colonel. From Saratoga, Col. Hutchins returned to domestic life, and died at Concord, December 8th, 1815, aged 82 years. He married two wives, and by them had twenty children.

Capt. NATHANIEL ABBOT.

Capt. NATHANIEL ABBOT was one of the earliest settlers of this place, and a very efficient citizen. He was born in 1696, at Andover. At the commencement of the French war, in 1744, he entered the service, and joined the Rangers under Major Rogers. He was at the capture of Cape Breton in 1745—was subsequently in most of the sanguinary conflicts on the northern frontiers ; and endured almost incredible hardships.* He held a commission in the corps of Rangers, and was in every station, a brave and useful officer. He died in 1770.†

Capt. JOSHUA ABBOT.

Capt. JOSHUA ABBOT, son of the preceding, accompanied his father during the latter part of his stay with the army. At the commencement of the revolutionary contest, he entered with zeal into the public service, and continued a firm and undeviating patriot to its close. He was a man of fine constitution, enjoying uninterrupted health, and he made every exertion in his power, in common with his compatriots in arms, for the achievement of our independence. He died in this town in 1815, aged 74.

Hon. JOHN BRADLEY.

The honorable JOHN BRADLEY was a son of Samuel Bradley, who was massacred by the Indians in 1746. He was about two years of age at the time of his father's death. He settled in his native town, and amongst her citizens was distinguished as one of the most enterprizing and useful. Possessing a sound mind, and great dignity of charac-

* A faithful picture has probably never yet been drawn of the species of warfare prosecuted by the Rangers—or of the hardships and privations endured by the soldiery in the old French wars. Mr. JOHN SHUTE, now living in this town, at the age of 89 years, and whose memory and faculties are unimpaired, was a soldier under Rogers in the ranging service ; and an hour spent in listening to his account of that service, and his own sufferings and adventures, is by no one regretted. Mr. S. is a son of Jacob Shute, who came with the first family of settlers to Penacook.

† *George Abbot*, the paternal ancestor of the families of that name. came out of England, and settled at Andover, Mass. about 1645, where he died Oct. 5, 1681. He had 10 sons and 3 daughters. *Nathaniel*, his youngest son, was born July 15, 1671 ; settled at Andover, and died Dec. 12, 1749. His son, *Nathaniel*, born in 1696, settled in Concord, and died in 1770. His son, *Joshua*, was born at Concord in 1741, and died in 1815. *Nathaniel Abbot*, his son, is now living in this town, and is of the fifth generation from Capt. George Abbot.

ter, as well as integrity of principle, he was frequently invited to public stations, and served in both branches of the legislature. In the discharge of his official, no less than his private duties, he was firm and consistent, acting independently, and according to his deliberate convictions of justice. He lived to a good old age, and died on the 5th day of July, in the year 1815.

Deacon JOHN KIMBALL.

Deacon JOHN KIMBALL was a native of Bradford, in Massachusetts, and born February 16, 1739. He settled here at an early period of his life, and soon became an active and valuable citizen. He discharged every official duty with promptness and fidelity, and in his private walks, was a pattern of christian meekness and charity. He was a member of the church for nearly sixty years, and sustained an office in the church in this place during about forty years. He died on the 31st of December, 1817, aged 79. He had been 'married 52 years, and reared a numerous family, during which time no death occurred beneath his roof. Mrs. Kimball, his wife, died March 5, 1819.

Lt. RICHARD HERBERT.

Lt. RICHARD HERBERT died on the 17th July, 1823, aged 94. His father, James Herbert, a ship-carpenter, was a native of England, married his wife in Rowley, and settled at Salisbury, where Richard was born December 31, 1729. Mr. Herbert came to this town in 1752, and purchased the first lot of land sold by the proprietors on the street.* He was industrious in business, and soon became a useful citizen. He was among the first volunteers†

---

*This lot consisted of about two acres, and was the ground owned by the late Capt. Dearborn. Mr. Herbert gave $10 dollars for his land, then apparently a sand-heap, and was frequently rallied by his neighbor land-holders for his singular purchase. He lived, however, to profit by its increase in value.

† The first person in Concord who accepted a commission under the provincial congress, was Capt. REUBEN KIMBALL. He was a zealous friend to the revolutionary cause—raised a company, and was at Saratoga, when the army of Burgoyne surrendered to the Americans. He died June 13, 1814, aged 84.

from this town in 1775—was an officer under Stark at the battle of Bennington, and proved himself a brave and useful man. After the victory, he returned to Concord, and spent the remainder of his life in industry, inoffensiveness and peace.

—»»○◉◦«—

Churches and Religious Societies.

It will be perceived, that among the first objects of the early settlers of Concord, was the settlement of a minister of the gospel. A church, consisting of eight individuals,* was formed on the 18th of November, 1730 ; at which time the Rev. Mr. Walker was ordained. Their place of public worship, was the log-house, erected in 1727, and used also as a garrison for refuge, in times of alarm and danger. Mr. Walker was a man well fitted to meet the sufferings and privations of the wilderness, and to build up, by sound precept and encouraging example, a united and prosperous church. He was a good farmer, an efficient citizen, and an exemplary christian. In common with his parishioners, he shared the difficulties of their situation, and met, without shrinking, every emergency of want or danger. The troubles which the inhabitants experienced from 1730 to 1770, seemed to have produced an habitual union, which continued for a long time after these troubles had ceased. During a period of more than eighty years, there were no visible differences among the people on religious subjects. For a few years previous to 1816, there had been a respectable society of Friends, who worshipped separately. In 1818, societies of Epis-

---

* *Names of those who formed the first congregational church in this place, embodied Nov. 18, 1730.*

Timothy Walker,	‖	William Barker,
John Merrill,	‖	David Barker,
Samuel Burbank,	‖	Aaron Stevens,
Jeremiah Stickney,	‖	John Russ.

copalians and Baptists were formed, the latter of which is still in a prosperous state.

Rev. Mr. Walker continued the pastor of the congregational church until his death in 1782. From this period until 1789, the church was without a minister, though the ordinances were pretty regularly administered and attended. Rev. Mr. Evans was installed in 1789; continued to preach until the summer of 1797, when his pastoral relation to the church was by mutual consent dissolved. The present incumbent, Rev. Dr. M'Farland, succeeded to the care of the church in 1798.

This church is independent in its form—its government agreeing with the principles of those who fled from persecution in England, to enjoy in this then inhospitable land their religious opinions. It admits the principle of a communion of churches according to the Cambridge platform; but it has never yet had occasion to call in the aid of other churches to settle difficulties. No ecclesiastical council has been called here, except for the purpose of ordaining or dismissing a minister. The church has a standing committee, whose duties are to assist the pastor in examining candidates for admission, and in endeavoring to settle difficulties, that may arise between individuals, without an appeal to the whole body of the church. Every member has a right to the judgment of the whole body; and, as a last resort, each has a right of appeal to a council of the neighboring churches.

This church, if not the largest, is one of the largest in the state—the number of communicants at present being about 340.

During the ministry of the Rev. Mr. Walker, the recorded admissions to the church are 34 males; 61 females—Total, 95; but this undoubtedly falls far below the actual number. Mr. Walker died in 1782; and of the admissions to the church during the ministry of his successor, Mr. Evans, from 1789 to 1797, no record can be found. The following table, drawn from the records of Rev. Dr. M'Farland, will shew at a glance the number of baptisms, marriages, and admissions to the church, since his ordination, in 1798.

YEARS.	1798	1799	1800	1801	1802	1803	1804	1805	1806	1807	1808	1809	1810	1811
Baptisms,*	34	21	16	17	24	12	16	13	14	20	24	21	15	92
Marriages,†	13	6	8	11	12	22	23	22	17	26	26	20	23	14
Admissions,‡	5	4	3	2	15	1	8	3	1	5	10	8	8	59

YEARS.	1812	1813	1814	1815	1816	1817	1818	1819	1820	1821	1822	1823	TOTALS.
Baptisms,	44	20	13	13	82	35	12	12	78	34	18	15	715
Marriages,	23	14	19	21	20	14	22	9	19	14	11	15	414
Admissions,	36	6	12	4	108	13	6	8	85	9	7	9	435

* There is a record of about 90 baptisms during the ministry of Rev. Mr. Evans, but probably imperfect.

† There are only 8 marriages by Rev. Mr. Walker, on record—those previous to 1738.

‡ This includes those admitted in the usual form, and such as were added by letters from other churches.

Deacons in the Congregational Church, since its organization in 1730.

John Merrill,
Ephraim Farnum,
George Abbot,
John Kimball,
David Hall,

Joseph Hall,
Jonathan Wilkins,
Abiel Rolfe,
Thomas W. Thompson,
Nathaniel Ambrose.

Topography.

This town comprises a tract of nearly 41,000 acres, of which 1800 are water. The surface is uneven, though it presents none of the rude acclivities or deep valleys seen in some of the neighboring towns. There are five ponds in Concord, two on the east of the Merrimack, and three on the west. The largest is Turkey pond, in the south-

70 ANNALS OF CONCORD.

west part of the town, containing about 700 acres ;
the waters of which form the Turkey river, a stream
of some importance, passing east into Bow. Long
pond, in the west part of the town, contains about
500 acres, the waters of which pass into the Merrimack below Sewall's island. Turtle pond lies east
of Long pond, and near the line of Loudon ; it contains about 200 acres, and its waters pass into the
Merrimack through the valley east of the river.
The others are Snow's pond, north-west of Turtle
pond, and Horse-shoe pond, near the meeting-
house. The river Soucook forms the south-east
boundary of Concord, from Chichester to its junction with the Merrimack below Garven's falls.
The Contoocook is a considerable river, entering
near the west corner of the town, and uniting with
the Merrimack on the north-west line, forming at
its junction the island celebrated as the spot where
Mrs. Duston made a desperate escape from a party
of Indians, in 1698. The design below presents a tolerably accurate view of the island,
though it rapidly changes in its appearance, from
the action of the freshes of the river.

The Merrimack is the principal river of this
region, and is not only the ornament and beautifier
of the landscape, but the source of health and
profit to the inhabitants. It meanders nearly
through the centre of the town, enriching the
tracts of interval on its borders. The intervals
here are of considerable width, and of great value

to the town; though perhaps inferior in extent and beauty to those on the Connecticut. Soon after entering the town, the Merrimack passes over the rapids called Sewall's falls, below which is situated Sewall's island, thus called from an early proprietor. The current of the river from this island is not rapid, and has no natural obstructions, until it reaches Turkey and Garven's falls at the south-east extremity of the town. Locks are here constructed, and the navigation of the river has been open during the boating seasons for several years. The river is here about 100 yards wide, but occasionally, the spring and autumn freshes have covered the interval adjoining the principal village, presenting to the eye a body of water of a mile in width. These freshes, though often destructive to crops, fences, &c. are of no disadvantage to the soil, on which they deposit a rich sediment. During the greatest freshes, the river has risen nearly 20 feet above the ordinary level, but this is uncommon. There are two bridges thrown across the river in this town : the Federal, or Upper Bridge, and Concord, or Lower Bridge. At these bridges, are situated the store-houses of the Boating Company on the river. The intercourse with Boston, opened by way of the canals on the Merrimack, has been of considerable advantage to the country. The navigation to this town was opened in 1815,* and the quantity of goods annually brought up has averaged 1000 to 1500 tons. The freight downward has been more extensive, consisting of the produce of the country, lumber, and other heavy or bulky articles. For the first three years, the business on the river exceeded that for the three last ; but there is a prospect that it will hereafter be much increased. The principal village, and the seat of most of the business of the town, extends along the western bank of the Merrimack nearly

*The first boat of the Merrimack company, arrived at the landing here, June 23, 1815, in 3 1-2 days from Boston.

two miles from south-east to north-west. It is very
pleasantly situated, and from its convenient situation
has become a place of considerable trade. The
state-house,* state-prison, court-house and meeting-
house are situated in this village. There are 175
dwelling-houses, 20 stores, 8 taverns, several me-
chanic shops, 5 printing-offices, 5 bookstores and 2
book-binderies. On the east side of the river, is
another considerable village, very pleasantly situated ; and a village is also forming in the west part
of the town. The soil of this town presents all
the varieties common to this region, and is in some
parts fertile. The highlands extending back from
the river are very productive, and were originally
covered with oak, chesnut, maple, &c. The plains are
alluvial, and covered with a growth of pine. Large
masses of excellent granite are found in this town,
and the public edifices here, are erected of this
material. This granite affords an admirable material for building ; and large quantities, wrought at
the State Prison, are annually transported to Boston for architectural purposes. It derives its supe-
riority over the granite of many other countries,
from the circumstance that it contains no sulphuret
of iron, which, by the action of atmospheric agents,
produces an iron-rust stain, that destroys the beauty of the material. Iron ore is found here in small
quantities, near the Soucook river, and on the
branches of the Turkey river. It was wrought by
the inhabitants during the revolution ; but to no
great extent. Excellent clay abounds in several
places, and extensive potteries have for some years
been established.

* See description of public buildings, p. 49.

Memoir of the Penacook Indians.

Whatever relates to the aboriginals of our country, those early proprietors of the soil which we inherit, must be interesting to posterity. The lands which we cultivate, the forests, the rivers and mountains around us, once swarmed with a distinct race of the human family. They whose character once stood so lofty and independent, are hardly seen among us, and if seen, are seen " begging the price of their perdition."—They who might have exterminated the Europeans on their arrival, have themselves become exterminated, and most of their memorials have perished with them. Much is it to be regretted, that there has been no historical account of the various tribes residing on Merrimack river, and particularly of the one inhabiting the town of Concord, known at an early period of our history as acknowledging allegiance to the far famed sachem, Passaconaway. But there have been causes why this has not been done. " The horror proceeding from the cruelties of their warfare, forbade the calmness of investigation. As long as they were formidable, curiosity was overpowered by terror ; and there was neither leisure, nor inclination to contemplate their character as a portion of the human family, while the glare of conflagration reddened the midnight sky, and the yells of the savage, mingling with the shrieks of butchered victims, rode, as portentous messengers, on every gale. But that state of things has long ceased to exist. The white men of America have become too numerous to fear any longer the effects of savage barbarity, and the tales which once carried terror to the stoutest heart, are now scarcely heard beyond the precincts of the nursery. In the room of fear, there should now arise a sentiment of pity."*

---

* Rev. Dr. Jarvis' address before the New-York Hist. Soc.

When our fathers arrived in this country, they
found within the confines of New England, five
principal nations of the Indians ; viz. the Pequots
inhabiting Connecticut ; the Narragansetts, who
inhabited Rhode-Island and the adjacent country ;
the Pawkunnawkutts, who lived on Nantucket,
Martha's Vineyard, and in Plymouth colony ; the
Massachusetts, who lived about Massachusetts bay;
and the Pawtucketts, who constituted the " fifth
and last great sachemship of Indians." " Their
country lieth north and north-east from Massachusetts, whose dominion reacheth as far as the English jurisdiction or colony of the Massachusetts,
doth now extend."*

To this general division, belonged the Penacooks,
or those Indians, who inhabited Concord, and the
country for many miles above and below on Merrimack river. There were several " smaller saga-
moreships" which were included under the national name of Pawtucketts—such as the Agawams,
Naamkeeks, Pascataquas, Accomintas and some
others. All these subordinate tribes formed originally but one great nation, and acknowledged sub-
jection to Passaconaway, who was called " the
great sachem of Penacook."

The Penacooks were probably among the most
powerful of these subordinate tribes, though their
history is but little known, and at this distance of
time, cannot be given with any degree of minute-
ness. Passaconaway was the first sagamore of
whom we find any account in our historians. If
the Wheelwright deed be not a forgery, he was living as early as 1629, and it appears from Hubbard's
narrative, that he was alive in 1660. In that year,
the Indians had a great dance and feast, on which
occasion, this powerful sagamore, being grown old,
made his farewell speech to his children and people, in which, as a dying man, he warned them to

---

* Gookin, in Coll. of Mass. Hist. Soc. Vol. 1, page 149, first series.

take heed how they quarrelled with their English neighbors; for though they might do them some damage, yet it would prove the means of their own destruction. He told them he had been a bitter enemy to the English, and by the arts of sorcery, had tried his utmost to hinder their settlement and increase, but could by no means succeed.

Wonolanset succeeded his father as sachem of Penacook, and observed his dying advice. When the war with Philip commenced in 1675, he withdrew himself with his people to some remote place, that they might not be drawn into the quarrel. The Penacooks appear to have maintained a friendly disposition so long as they were under the control of Wonolanset.

About the year 1684, Lieut. Gov. Cranfield formed the project of bringing down the Mohawks, from New-York, in order to destroy the Penacook and Eastern Indians. This measure had once before been resorted to, but proved very pernicious in its effects, as that ferocious and warlike people made no distinction between those tribes which were at peace with the English, and those which were at war. Some of the Penacook Indians, who had been to Albany soon after Cranfield made a journey to the province of New-York, reported on their return, that the Mohawks threatened destruction to all the eastern Indians, from Narraganset in Rhode-Island to Pechypscot in Maine.* The Penacooks were about this time under the government of Hogkins, a sachem who succeeded Wonolanset. From the articles of Peace between the English inhabiting the province of N. Hampshire and Maine, and the Indians of these provinces, agreed upon the 8th day of September, 1685, it appears, that Kancamagus was his Indian name, and that Hog-

* " Four Indians came from fort Albany to the Fort at Pennicooke and informed them that all the Mokawkes did declare they would kill all Indians from Uncas at Mount Hope to the eastward as far as Pegypscut." *Report to Walter Barefoote. Esq. and Council.*

kins or Hawkins was the English name he had assumed.

In the spring of 1685, he informed Cranfield of the danger the Penacooks apprehended,* and implored assistance and protection, but was treated with neglect.

In August, 1685, the Penacook and Saco Indians gathered their corn, and removed their families, which gave an alarm to their English neighbors, as if they were preparing for war. Messengers being sent to demand the reason of their movement, were informed that it was the fear of Mohawks, whom they daily expected to destroy them; and being asked why they did not come in among the English for protection, they answered, lest the Mohawks should hurt the English on that account. Upon this, they were persuaded to enter into an agreement; and accordingly the chiefs of the Penacooks and of the Saco Indians being assembled with the Council of New-Hampshire, and a deputation from the province of Maine, a treaty was concluded, wherein it was stipulated, that all future personal injuries on either side should, upon

---

* His letter to Gov. Cranfield at this time will explain his situation and his fears, and may be regarded as a curiosity. The original is preserved in the Recorder's office in N. H.

May 15th, 1685.

" *Honour gouernor my friend,*

You my friend I desire your worship and your power, because I hope you can do som great matters this one. I am poor and naked, and I have no man at my place because I afraid allwayes Mohogs he will kill me every day and night. If your worship when please pray help me you no let Mohogs kill me at my place at Malamake river called Panukkog and Nattukkog, I will submit your worship and your power. And now I want pouder and such alminishon, shott and guns, because I have forth at my hom and I plant theare.

This all Indian hand, but pray do you consider your humble servant,

JOHN HOGKINS.

Simon Detogkom,	Peter ꞓ Robin,
Joseph X Traske,	Mr Jorge + Roddunnonukgus,
King ‖ Hary,	Mr Hope X Hoth,
Sam ‖ Linis, [at,	John + Tonch,
Wapeguanal ‖ Saguachuwash,	John ā Canowa,
Old Robin ‖	John x Owamosimmin,
Mamanosgues ꞓ Andra,	Naionill † Indian."

These were probably some of the principal men of the tribe. Two other letters from Hogkins to Cranfield are preserved in I. Belknap, 346.

complaint, be immediately redressed ; that information should be given of approaching danger from enemies ; that the Indians should not remove their families from the neighborhood of the English without giving timely notice, and if they did, it should be taken for a declaration of war ; and, that while these articles were observed, the English would assist and protect them against the Mohawks and all other enemies.

From this time, peace continued without interruption till 1689, when a confederacy was formed between the tribes of Penacook and Pequawkett, and the strange Indians, (as they were called) who were incorporated with them, to attack the settlement at Dover. The Penacooks were among the four hundred Indians, who were seized at Dover by Major Waldron in 1676, and were dismissed at that time, probably on account of the friendly disposition of Wonolanset. Notwithstanding they experienced the clemency of Major Waldron, in being permitted to depart in safety, they did not *forget* the conduct of the Major to their allies, and were easily seduced to join the confederacy by those, who had, for about thirteen years, cherished an inextinguishable thirst of revenge against the brave, but unfortunate Waldron. The plot formed against the inhabitants of Dover was disclosed by two of the Penacooks to Major Hinchman, of Chelmsford, who immediately informed Mr. Danforth, a member of the council of Massachusetts, by the following letter, the original of which is on file in the Secretary's office in Massachusetts.

" *Hon'd Sir*,

This day, two Indians came from Pennacook, viz. Job Maramasquand and Peter Muckamug, who report that damage will undoubtedly be done within a few days at Piscataqua, and that Major Waldron, in particular, is threatened ; and that Julimatt fears that mischief will quickly be done at

11

Dunstable. The Indians can give a more particular account to your honor. They say, if damage be done, the blame shall not be on them, having given a faithful account of what they hear ; and are upon that report moved to leave their habitation and corn at Pennacook. Sir, I was very loth to trouble you, and to expose myself to the censure and derision of some of the confident people, that would pretend to make a sport with what I send down by Capt. Tom, (alias Thomas Ukqucakussennum.)

I am constrained, from a sense of my duty, and from love to my countrymen, to give the information as above. So with my humble service to your honor, and prayers for the safety of an endangered people—I am, Sir, your humble servant,

THO: HINCHMAN.

June 22.

Hon. Thomas Danforth."

Mr. Danforth was detained from the meeting of the council. He however, on the same day, communicated Major Hinchman's letter to Governor Bradstreet, who, with the council, ordered a messenger to be sent to Cochecho, with the following disclosure of the plot in a letter, written by Secretary Addington.

"*Boston*, 27 *June*, 1689.

Honble Sir,

The governor and councill haveing this day received a letter from Major Henchman of Chelmsford, that some Indians are come in to them, who report that there is a gathering of some Indians in and about Penecooke, with designe of mischiefe to the English. Among the said Indians, one Hawkins is said to be a principal designer, and that they have a particular designe against yourself and Mr. Peter Coffin, which the councill thought it necessary presently to dispatch advice thereof to give you notice, that you take care of your own safeguard, they intending to betray you on a pretention of trade.

Please forthwith to signify the import hereof to Mr. Coffin and others, as you shall think necessary, and advise of what informations you may at any time receive of the Indians motions. By order in Councill. ISA : ADDINGTON, *Sec'y*.

For Mr. Richard Waldron and Mr. Peter
Coffin, or either of them, att Cochecha ;
these with all possible speed."

This letter was despatched from Boston by Mr. Weare; but some delay he met with at Newbury ferry prevented its arrival in season. The same day, after the mischief was done, the preceding letter fell into the hands of Maj. Waldron's son. Had it been seasonably received, it would probably have saved the lives of twenty-three persons, who fell a sacrifice to Indian cruelty, besides preventing the capture of twenty-nine others, and the destruction of much valuable property.*

Upon the depredations at Dover, vigorous measures were immediately adopted. A party under Capt. Noyes was despatched to Penacook, to inflict summary punishment upon those who were concerned in the affair at Cochecho ; but the Indians all escaped. They, however, destroyed their corn.

It appears that after this, the Penacooks continued to exist as a distinct tribe for many years ; though as a separate tribe, they ceased to be formidable after this event. We find that they are mentioned in Penhallow's Indian Wars, (page 2,) where there is an account of a conference held by Governor Dudley at Casco, in 1703, with delegates from several tribes. The Norridgewocks, Penobscots, Pequawketts, Penacooks and Ameriscoggins assured the governor, at this meeting, that " as high as the sun was above the earth, so far distant was

---

* For a particular account of the attack on Dover, see Belknap's His. N. H. vol. I, page 198.

their design of making the least breach of the
peace."

At the same time they made this declaration, they
were meditating hostilities, which commenced on
the 10th of August, 1703. After this period, we
hear little or nothing of the Penacooks, as a separate tribe. Those of them who were hostile to the
English, probably mixed with the eastern Indians,
between whom and the Penacooks, was a close af-
finity. As the governor of Canada had encouraged
the Indians who inhabited the borders of New-
England, to remove to Canada, it is likely that
some of them went thither, and were incorporated
with the tribes of St. Francis. But those who continued friendly to the English, of which there had
always been a small number, remained here until
1725, and were highly useful to the first inhabitants,
supplying them with food when almost in a state
of starvation.

The Penacook Indians were a more warlike tribe
than the Pawtuckett, or Wamesit Indians, who lived around Pawtuckett Falls, in Chelmsford. They
were opposed to the introduction of christianity a-
mong them, and "obstinately refused to pray to
God." Before the year 1670, a party of them went
down the Merrimack, and built a fort at Pawtuckett. They also erected a fort on Sugar-Ball Hill,
so called, in Concord, as a protection against the
incursions of the Mohawks and other enemies. A
considerable number of them joined in an expedition against that formidable nation, and were principally destroyed. Tradition says, that there was
once a very obstinate engagement between the Mohawks and Penacooks on the river in this vicinity,
but the time, place and circumstances are unknown
to the present generation. The Indians of the most
peaceful character among the Penacooks, were the
Robin family, a part of which lived in Chelmsford,
and owned a hill in that town, which, for almost
two hundred years, has been known by the name of
Robin's Hill.

APPENDIX.

—»»●●●««—

[NO. I.]

THE ORDER OF THE GREAT AND GENERAL COURT.

The Committee appointed to consider what is proper for this Court to do on the petition of Benjamin Stevens and others, are humbly of opinion, that it will be for the interest and advantage of this Province that part of the lands, petitioned for by the said Benjamin Stevens and company, be assigned and set apart for a township ; provided, that the same be done in a good, regular and defensible manner, to contain seven miles square, and begin where Contoocook river falls into Merrimack river, and thence to extend upon a course east seventeen degrees south four miles, to be the northerly bounds of the said township ; and from the extreme parts of that line to be set off southerly at right angles, until seven miles shall be accomplished from the said north bounds. And that the petitioners may be encouraged and fully empowered to prosecute their intended settlements—Ordered, That the Hon. William Tailer, Esq., Elisha Cooke, Esq.,Spencer Phipps, Esq., William Dudley, Esq., John Wainwright, Esq., Capt. John Shipley, Mr. John Saunders, Eleazar Tyng, Esq., and Mr. Joseph Wilder, (any five of whom to be a quorum) be a Committee to take special care, that the following rules and conditions be punctually observed and kept by all such as shall be admitted to bring forward the proposed settlements, namely :

That the aforesaid tract of land be allotted and divided into one hundred and three equal parts and shares as to quantity and quality ; and that one hundred persons or families, such only as in the judgment of the Committee shall be well able to pursue and bring to pass their several settlements on the said lands within the space of three years at farthest from the first day of June next. That each and every intended settler, to whom a lot, with the rights and privileges thereto belonging, shall be assigned, shall pay into the hands of the Committee, for the use of the Province, at the time of drawing his lot, the sum of five pounds, and be obliged to build a good dwelling house, fit comfortably to receive and entertain a family who shall inhabit the same ; and also break up and sufficiently fence in six acres of land for their home lot within the term aforesaid. And that the first fifty settlements shall be begun and perfected upon the eastern side of the said river Merrimack, and the several houses shall be erected on their home lots not above twenty rods the one from the other where the land will possibly admit thereof, in the most regular and defensible manner, the Committee, in their best prudence, can project and order ; the houses and home lots on

each side of the river to be alike subjected unto the above mentioned conditions.   That a convenient house for the public worship of God be completely finished within the term aforesaid,
for the accommodation of all such as shall inhabit the aforesaid
tract of land,upon such part thereof as shall be agreed upon by the
said Committee, for the ease of the community ; and that there
shall be reserved, allotted, and laid out for the first minister that
shall be lawfuly settled among them, one full right, share, and
proportion of and in the aforesaid tract of land, with all rights
and privileges thereto belonging.   His house lot to be laid out
next adjoining to the land whereon the meeting house shall
stand.   One other full right, share, and proportion of and in the
aforesaid tract of land, to be appropriated for the use of the
school forever ; and one other ministerial lot of equal value
with the rest, the home lot appertaining thereto affixed near to
the meeting house.   And for the better enabling the intended
settlers to perfect what they are hereby enjoined, and empowering them to remove all such lets and impediments as they may
meet with in their progress and lawful undertaking, that when
and so soon as there shall be one hundred persons accepted and
allowed by the Committee to go on and improve those lands for
the ends and uses above specified, upon application made to the
aforesaid Committee, it shall and may be lawful for them to no-
tify the undertakers to meet at some convenient time and place,
they being seasonably notified of such meeting, who, when assembled, shall make such necessary rules and orders as to them
shall be thought most conducible for the carrying forward and
effecting the aforesaid settlement ; provided, that three-fourth
parts of the persons present at such meeting are consenting to
what rules or orders shall be then proposed and agreed upon,
two or more of the Committee to be present at such meeting,
who shall enter into a fair book, to be kept for that purpose, all
such rules, orders, and directions agreed on as aforesaid, and give
out copies thereof when required ; the whole charge of the
Committee to be paid by the settlers.   And that when they shall
have performed the conditions above expressed, provided it be
within the space of three years as before limited, that then the
said Committee for and in behalf of this Court execute good and
sufficient deeds and conveyances in the law, to all such settlers
for the aforesaid tract of land, with all the rights, members,
profits, privileges, and immunities thereon standing, growing, or
being for the sole use of them, their heirs and assigns forever,
with a saving of all or any former grant or grants.
      By order of the Committee.
                                        N. BYFIELD.
      In Council, January 17th, 1725.   Read and ordered that this
Report be accepted.
      Sent down for concurrence.
                              J. WILLARD, Sec'ry.

In the House of Representatives, January 17th, 1725. Read and concurred.

WM. DUDLEY, Speaker.

Consented to,

WM. DUMMER.

[NO. II.]

Names of the Original Proprietors of the town of Rumford.

Nathaniel Abbot
John Austin
Samuel Ayer
John Ayer
Jacob Abbot
Obadiah Ayer
Zebadiah Barker, alias Edw. Abbot
Thomas Blanchard
William Barker
Nathaniel Barker, alias Solo. Martin
Joshua Bayley
Moses Boardman
Nathan Blodgett
John Bayley, alias Samuel White
Nathaniel Clement
John Chandler
Benjamin Carlton
Christopher Carlton
Nehemiah Carlton
Richard Coolidge, alias Samuel Jones
John Coggin
Edward Clark
Enoch Coffin
Thomas Coleman
Nathaniel Cogswell
Moses Day
Joseph Davis
Samuel Davis
David Dodge
Ephraim Davis
Ebenezer Eastman
Jacob Eames
Stephen Emerson
John Foster
Ephraim Farnum

William Foster
Nathan Fisk, alias Zachariah Chandler
John Grainger
Samuel Grainger
Benjamin Gage
William Gutterson
Nehemiah Heath
Ephraim Hildreth
Joseph Hale
Moses Hazzen
Jonathan Hubbard, alias Daniel Davis
Richard Hazzen
Joseph Hall
Timothy Johnson
John Jaques
Nathaniel Jones
Robert Kimball
Samuel Kimball
David Kimball
Nathaniel Lovejoy
Ebenezer Lovejoy
Thomas Learned
John Merrill
John Mattis
Andrew Mitchel Minister
Benjamin Nichols
John Osgood
Stephen Osgood
Benjamin Parker
Thomas Page
Robert Peaslee
Joseph Parker
Nathan Parker
Nathaniel Page
Samuel Phillips
James Parker

Jonathan Pulsipher
Nathaniel Peaslee
John Pecker
Joseph Page
John Peabody
Parsonage
Samuel Reynolds
Henry Rolfe
John Sanders
Ebenezer Stevens
John Sanders, jr.
Benjamin Stevens
Nathaniel Saunders
James Simonds
Zorobabel Snow
Jonathan Shipley

Nathan Simonds
School
Samuel Tappan
Bezaleel Tappan
Richard Urann
Ebenezer Virgin
John Wright
William White
Nicholas White
Ammi Ruhamah Wise
Isaac Walker
David Wood
William Whittier
Thomas Wicomb
Edward Winn.

[NO. III.]

To His Excellency Benning Wentworth, Esq. Captain General and Governor in Chief in and over his Majesty's Province of New-Hampshire, in New-England, the Honorable the Council, and the House of Representatives, in General Court convened.

The Memorial and Petition of Benjamin Rolfe, in the name and behalf of the inhabitants of the town of Rumford, in said Province, humbly sheweth—That the said town has been settled by his Majesty's subjects about seventeen years, and a gospel minister ordained there about twelve. That the settlers had an eye at enlarging his Majesty's dominions, by going into the wilderness, as well as at their own interest. That many thousand pounds have been spent in clearing and cultivating the lands there, and many more in erecting mansion-houses, out-houses, barns, and fences ; besides a large additional sum in fortifications, lately made by his Excellency the Governor's order. That the buildings are compact, and properly formed for defence, and well situated for a barrier, being on the Merrimack river, about fifteen miles below the confluence of Winnipishoky [Winnepisiogee] and Pemissawasset [Pemigewasset] rivers, both which are main gang-ways of the Canadians to the frontiers of this Province. That the breaking up of the settlement will not only ruin the memorialists, but in their humble opinion, greatly disserve his Majesty's interest, by encouraging his enemies to encroach on his direlict dominions, and be all-hurtful to the Province, by contracting its borders, and by drawing the war nearer to the capital. That it was by a long and importunate intercession of this Province, (and not of the memorialists' seeking) that they are cast under the immediate care of this government, which, they apprehend, gives them so much the better right to its protection. That the memorialists have hitherto cheerfully paid their proportionate part of the public taxes assigned them by the general court, even without being privileged with a representative in said court. That, as war is already declared against France, and a rupture with the Indians hourly expected, your memorialists, unless they have speedy help, will be soon obliged to evacuate their town, how disserviceable soever it may be to the Crown, dishonorable to the government, hurtful to the Province, and ruinous to themselves. Wherefore your memorialists most humbly supplicate your Excellency, the Honorable Council, and House of Representatives, to take the premises into your wise and mature consideration, and to grant them such seasonable relief as may enable them to maintain his Majesty's dominions in so well situated a barrier, and so ancient and well regulated a settlement, as well as to secure their own lives and fortunes against the ravages and devastations of a blood-thirsty and merciless enemy. And your memorialists, as in duty bound, &c.

(Signed)   BENJAMIN ROLFE.

Portsmouth, June 27, 1744.

[NO. IV.]

To His Excellency Benning Wentworth, Esq. Governor and Commander in Chief in and over His Majesty's Province of New-Hampshire, in New-England, and to the Honorable His Majesty's Council of said Province.

The Memorial of Benjamin Rolfe, in the name and behalf of the inhabitants of Rumford, in said Province, humbly sheweth, That your memorialists are settled on a tract of land granted by the General Court of the Province of the Massachusetts Bay, in New-England, Anno Domini, 1725, and that the said tract of land was erected into a township by an act of said General Court, Anno Domini, 1733. The bounds of said township being as follows, viz. : Beginning where Contoocook river falls into Merrimack river, and thence to extend upon a course east seventeen degrees north three miles, and upon a course west seventeen degrees south four miles, which is the northerly bounds of the said township ; and from the other parts of that line to be set off southerly at right angles until seven miles and one hundred rods shall be accomplished from the said northern bounds. And that his Majesty in Council taking the said act into consideration, Anno Domini, 1737, was graciously pleased to declare his approbation thereof ; and by the late settlement of the boundaries between the said Provinces, by his Majesty in Council, the said township is within this Province. And by an act of the General Assembly of this Province, of March 18th, 1741-2, Rumford aforesaid was made a district, it not being incorporated within any township or parish within this Province ; and by said act your memorialists were subjected to pay a tax towards the support of this government, which they have punctually and cheerfully done every year since, pursuant to acts of this government. And your memorialists, by power given them by the district acts, so called, for about six years last past, have annually raised money for defraying our ministerial, school, and other necessary charges of said Rumford, and taxed the inhabitants accordingly ; but the district act expiring sometime last summer, there is now no law of this Province whereby your memorialists can raise any money for the year current, for the charges aforesaid. And your memorialists have abundant reason to think that the Rev. Mr. Timothy Walker, who has been settled with us as our minister for about twenty years, (unless we can speedily be put into a capacity to make a tax for his salary) will be necessitated to leave us, which will be to our great loss and inexpressible grief ; for he is a gentleman of an unspotted character, and universally beloved by us. Our public school will also of course fail, and our youth thereby be deprived, in a great measure, of the means of learning, which we apprehend to be of a very bad consequence. Our school-master, who is a gentleman of a liberal education, and came well recommended to us, and lately moved his family from Andover to Rumford, on account of his keeping school for us, will be greatly damaged and disappointed. And your memorialists, under their present circumstances, are deprived of all other privileges which a well regulated town (as such) enjoy.

Your memorialists, therefore, most humbly pray, that your Excellency and Honors would take our deplorable circumstances into your wise and mature consideration, and afford us relief by incorporating us into a township by our ancient boundaries as aforesaid, and by endowing of us with such privileges as any of the towns in this Province by law do or ought to enjoy. And your memorialists as in duty bound shall ever pray.

BENJAMIN ROLFE.

Portsmouth, January 24, 1749.

[NO. V.]

Documents relating to the Controversy between the Proprietors of Rumford and Bow.

THE STATE OF THE CASE,

Lately decided at the Superior Court of New-Hampshire, between The Proprietors of Bow, Plfs. and John Merrill, Def. [1750.]

The action was ejectment brought by said proprietors against him for the recovery of about eight acres of land, situate in Bow, and particularly described in their writ, with the buildings and appurtenances thereof, to the inferior court of common pleas, holden at Portsmouth, December, 1750, and at the defendant's request continued to the next term of said court, he being a purchaser of part of the land he holds, to vouch in his warrantor. But as he did not appear, the said John was obliged to defend himself, or give up the land demanded, on which some of his buildings stand. He therefore gave an issuable plea, and thereupon obtained judgment, from which the plaintiffs appealed to the then next superior court, entered their appeal, and after several continuances, parties had an hearing, and judgment was rendered for the plaintiffs to recover the premises demanded. This judgment the defendant reviewed. But judgment was again rendered for the plaintiffs. From which judgment he would have appealed to the king in council, or to the governor and council here in a court of appeals ; but both were denied, as the premises demanded were not of sufficient value to allow either, according to the province law in such cases. But as there is much more than what is of value sufficient to allow either of those appeals, depending upon the same title, the defendant is aggrieved at the denial as well as at the judgment he would have appealed from. It is proposed here to take notice of the most remarkable things offered by each party. But as it is a known rule in these cases, that the plaintiff must recover (if at all) by the strength of his own title, and not by the weakness or defect of the defendant's, it may not be amiss more particularly to consider the title of these plaintiffs and the objections made against it on the part of the defendant ; and then briefly to mention the defendant's title, and the objections the plaintiffs offer to that, with what is said in behalf of the defendant in reply to those objections.

The plaintiffs urge, that the right to all the lands in the province was originally in the crown. That by a special clause in the governor's commissions for this province, from time to time, they were authorised to grant these lands to the inhabitants, with the advice of the council, in order to the regular settlement thereof. That in the absence of the chief governor, this power, with others contained in the commission, devolved upon the lieutenant-governor. That under the commission to governor Shute, this happened to be the case. And in his absence the late lieutenant-governor Wentworth, being commander in chief, on the 20th of May, 1727, at Portsmouth, with the advice of the council, by a charter of that date, granted to sundry of his Majesty's subjects, then inhabitants of the province, whose names were contained in a schedule annexed, a tract of land in said province, bounded as follows, viz. : " Beginning on the southeast side of the town of Chichester, and running nine miles by Chichester and Canterbury, and carrying that breadth of nine miles from each of the aforesaid towns south-west, until the full complement of eighty-one square miles are fully made up," with sundry privileges and limitations therein. That about twenty months after the date of this charter, a committee of the grantees entered, surveyed the land granted, and marked out the bounds, as appears by a return under their hands, in what manner they proceeded. And this transaction, they say, gave the grantees the actual seisin and possession of the whole. Though they also say, that this as to the purpose of giving them the seisin, is *ex abundanti*, for the grantees by operation of law, were seized immediately upon the executing their charter. But this entry and survey were especially designed that they might know and distinguish their township from others. That as they were thus seized of the whole by consequence of the premises demanded, as these are confessed to be within the aforesaid bounds. That about five years after this, they enclosed a parcel of this land, on the easterly side of Merrimack river, by conjecture about three miles square. All which facts, they prove by sundry testimonies in the case. Four of which amount to nothing more of any consequence than is declared in the return of the said survey. But take them altogether, the plaintiffs allege, they prove an actual entry on and possession of part, which they say is constructively a possession of the whole, and that continued so for the term of five or six years; and from that time to this, (about a year) they have been improving of part of said land, which gives them a right to oust any person, who has entered and possesses any part within the bounds of their charter, in any other right or claim.

What they further offer, is either by way of reply to the defendant's objections, or as objections to the defendant's title.

Now to this title the defendant objects, and urges sundry considerations. In the first place he submitted, and would again, upon a new trial, be glad to submit the point to be adjudged, whether the plaintiffs have proved their declaration. They declare, " that on the 12th day of June, 1727, they were seized of the premises, with others their common lands in said town of Bow, in fee, taking the profits thereof to the value, &c. and continued to be so seized thereof for one year then next ensuing, and ought now to have quiet and peaceable possession thereof ; yet the said John, within 23 years last past hath, without judgment of law, entered into the premises demanded, disseized the plaintiffs thereof," &c. To say nothing of the peculiarity of this declaration, the seisin which the plaintiffs allege they had, must mean (if it has any meaning) a seisin in fact, for no person ever took the profits by virtue of a seisin in law only. Now they never sat a foot on the lands contained within the bounds of their charter, till the aforesaid survey, and how their seisin on the 12th of June is proved by an entry above twenty months after, is difficult to conceive. Besides this, the settlers of the plantation, called Pennicoke, which comprehends the lands in question, had been in possession of it above a year before the date of this charter, (as will appear beyond dispute, when we consider the defendant's title,) at present, only observe what is proved by sundry testimonies produced by the defendant, viz. That the April and May before the date of Bow charter, there were fifty men at work on the said plantation, clearing land, hewing timber for a meeting-house, and pursuing other measures, in order to settle a town there. That they prosecuted the affair with such vigor, as to have a minister ordained and a church gathered in the year 1730. But they were clearing the land there almost two years before any of the proprietors of Bow had seen *their* land ; and all *they* did, when they entered, was only to run a chain, and mark some trees, at a great distance, round these laborers. They never so much as saw the land now demanded, where the settlers of Pennicoke were at work. And it appears, that *they* began to clear the land in question, when they first entered, because it is one of their house-lots, or home-lots, as they are commonly called, and in the nature of the thing, that should be first done. This possession has been continued without interruption to this day ; and indeed may well be computed (by the plaintiffs' rule of possessing land by walking round it) from two years before April above mentioned.

Now upon these facts, concerning the manner of entry and possession of these parties, it is easy to see with what propriety the plaintiffs could declare upon their own seisin ; and with what regard to truth it can be said to be proved.

But to proceed. Upon supposition the lands which the plaintiffs claim were the King's, at the time their charter was made, (which was not the case in fact) yet the plaintiffs have not derived that right to themselves, for this obvious reason—The Governor's authority to grant the King's lands was limited by the right of jurisdiction, and *that*, by the commission to that part of the province of New-Hampshire, lying and extending itself from three miles northward of Merrimack river, or any part thereof, to the province of Maine, (now the county of York) which is the easterly boundary of the commission. The westerly boundary of which, is the line running three miles northward of Merrimack as aforesaid. Now the land demanded by the plaintiffs in this suit lies on the westerly side of Merrimack river, more than three miles without the Governor's jurisdiction, by this commission, and consequently, he had no power to grant it ; for if it should be supposed he might grant the King's lands, out of his jurisdiction, where should he stop ? by what limits could he be restrained ? From the reason and necessity of the thing, therefore, it must be allowed, that the right of government, and the granting of lands was limited to the same territory. And the words of the commission necessarily imply, it did not extend over *all* that was called New-Hampshire. If it is conceded, then, that these lands are within the province of New-Hampshire, and were so at the date of the plaintiffs' charter, yet that concession will avail the plaintiffs nothing in this case.

Another objection to the plaintiffs' demand arises from the manner of their running out the bounds of their township. By their charter they were to begin on the south-east side of the township of Chichester. Instead of that, they began on the south-*west* side, as their return sets forth. Now what could justify their proceeding in this manner ? If the land where they

were to begin was appropriated before, that could not authorize
them to be their own carvers, to take what they are pleased to
estimate an equivalent, without a new grant, which they never
had, nor did they ever make a return to the authority from
whence they derived their title, for confirmation of what they
had thus unwarrantably assumed ; for by their running, they take
in a considerable tract of land, really without their charter, and
which belongs to others. And if there was a mistake to their
prejudice in the bounds given them, that is no new thing—the
King himself is sometimes deceived in his grants. In such a
case they should have applied to the grantor for redress. They
allege they could not begin on the south-east side of Chichester,
because it joined to Nottingham on that side ; but if it was so,
what necessity of going four miles on Chichester before they
began their measure ? Their return, indeed, says, they were
directed to leave four miles, &c. ; this is no more than their own
tale, for nothing appears to discover by whom, when, or where,
this direction was given. But a verbal direction was not sufficient in this case ; they should have taken their land according
to their grant ; and 'tis as probable as any thing they say as to
this matter, the true motive for making this leap, (not in the
dark) was to get better land. Now the defendant avers it to be
fact, that if they had run as they ought, from the southerly corner of Chichester, they would not have reached the land demanded.

But now to come closer to this title, as derived from the
Crown, the defendant says that the right to all the lands the plaintiffs claim as contained in their charter, was long before granted
by the council of Plymouth, in whom the right of the Crown to
them was vested, to Capt. John Mason, (if there had been no
preceding grant from said council) which was confirmed by King
Charles I., and has been recognized by every crowned head to
King George I., from whose time till lately nothing was said of
it, by reason of the absence or minority of the heir. By all
which it appears that this right of Mason was always adjudged
good. Now as the said lands were all waste or unimproved, except what the settlers at Pennicoke had done upon that which
they claimed of them, they, beyond all question, belonged (agreeable to Queen Anne's orders and the concession of the Assembly
here) to those who had Mason's right. And if this was the case,
the Governor's grant could be of none effect as to these lands ;
for the power of the Governor extends only to the right of the
Crown, of which the Crown was long before divested. Hence it
follows, the plaintiffs' title under the government cannot serve
them, of which the defendant may take advantage ; for it is a
well known rule that a defendant may plead any man's title
against the plaintiff.

And here the plaintiffs agree with the defendant, and allow the
right was Mason's, and that they cannot avail themselves of the
charter aforesaid, only as a description of what they claimed, and

were in possession of; but say, *they have that right,* for that Mr. Mason's heir sold to Theodore Atkinson, Esq. and others, by deed, dated the 30th of July, 1746, and that the purchasers, by their deed of release, dated 31st of July aforesaid, conveyed their right to the plaintiffs, among others. And here the defendant, not willing to be in arrears, will in his turn at present agree with the plaintiffs, that they have Mason's right to their lands, and make no question whether the right of Capt. John Mason is now in *his* heirs or Allen's. But then must quere how a right, acquired in 1746, could give an actual seisin of the lands, the right to which was then purchased, so long before the purchase as 1727 ; that is, whether a man, by virtue of a deed made to-day, could be in actual possession of the land conveyed by it nineteen years ago ? Moreover, the defendant must deny a right was conveyed by this release to the lands demanded, and whatever else is within the bounds of Rumford, that is the plantation of Pennicoke, for this reason. It is common learning on this subject, that a release operates only to those in possession, and the plaintiffs' own declaration shows they have been out of possession above twenty years. What benefit then have the plaintiffs by this release as to the lands aforesaid ?

But now if we look into the release, we shall find it is made as much to the defendant as any person whomsoever. For he is an inhabitant of Bow, as the plaintiffs themselves style him, and this release is made to the inhabitants as well as to proprietors, of what they possess ; and as the defendant had possessed so long in his own right, he must of necessity be quieted by this release, if it has any effect at all, and it would be doing the greatest violence to the words of it, to give them any other construction as to this point ; and if so, it is submitted whether the plaintiffs or defendant has Mason's right. But what may further be objected to the plaintiffs on this head, and indeed is what first occurs, it is a well known point of law, a chose in action or a mere right cannot be transferred, and Mason's title was no more, as to all the lands in the possession of those who were not parties at the time of making the said deed to Atkinson and others. The lands demanded, as well as all the plantation of Pennicoke, had been near twenty years in the possession of entire strangers to that transaction. And then what title can the plaintiffs derive to themselves under this conveyance to the lands in question ? This, and much more, the defendant conceives may well be offered in his defence, sufficient to defeat the plaintiffs' action, upon supposition he had no title. But that is not the case.—We shall now consider the defendant's title.

In the year 1725, upon the petition of Benjamin Stevens and others, a tract of land of seven miles square, at a place called Pennicoke, by the government of the Massachusetts Bay, was appropriated for a township, the bounds of which were as follows, viz. " To begin where Contoocoke river falls into Merrimack river, thence extending east seventeen degrees north three miles, and west seventeen degrees south four miles, which is the northerly bound of said township ; and from the extreme parts of that line southerly at right angles till seven miles are accomplished from the north bounds." Now it is agreed on all hands, that within these bounds the lands demanded are contained. And as the proprietors of Bow have run the bounds of the lands they claim, they take in something more than two-thirds of what is contained within the bounds above described. And, therefore, as they have recovered part, they expect to recover the whole that lies within what they are pleased to call their limits ; for other parcels of which there are several other actions now pending. And here it may not be amiss to take notice of the vexatious method they take to recover what they claim, by prosecuting a great number of actions, each for a small parcel of land, that they may prevent an appeal home, and that they may have the advantage of the ignorance and prejudice of common juries. And with a view to weary out and dishearten the defendants, who live at a great distance from Portsmouth, where all the courts are held, with the expense of charges occasioned to them by such a number of suits. Whereas they might as well have taken an action for all that lies in common, in the name of the proprietors of Bow, against the proprietors of Rumford, as well as the action against the present defendant, and others of the like kind. But to return. Among those who were to settle this town, is the name of the defendant and one Nathaniel Page, under whom he purchased a part of what is sued for. In the year 1726, a division of lots of upland and interval was laid out to the settlers, to hold in severalty, among which was the land demanded, part of which is that the defendant purchased of one Joseph Davis. These settlers prosecuted the settlement with such vigor, that in the year 1730 they had a minister settled, and a church gathered in said township. And in the year 1733, they were incorporated into a town, by the name of Rumford, (it not being the custom in this government to incorporate a tract of waste land without an inhabitant, but first to settle the land, and then make the settlers a corporation.) The act, by which this corporation was made, was confirmed by the King afterwards, in the year 1737. And notwithstanding their distance from other settlements, within, and none without them, the difficulties and hardships which necessarily attend those who first set down upon land in a perfect wilderness, where there is not the least sign that ever English foot had trod the ground before them ; and especially the danger, expense, and fatigue of an Indian war, which they encountered.* Notwithstanding all these and other discouragements, these settlers have stood their ground ever since their first entry ; have persevered in their resolution, have planted a fine town, supply themselves and many

---

* Besides an actual war, they have been frequently driven into garrisons, and kept in continual fears for years together, or at least the whole summer season, which was occasioned again the next, by the threats and surly temper of the Indians.

others within them with provisions, afford other places both defence and sustenance, and are likely to be a great advantage to the province of New-Hampshire in general. Yet these are the people the proprietors of Bow would eject ; would oust, not only of their all, but of *that all* they have thus dearly purchased. For what the said proprietors claim takes in all (within a very trifle) of the said improvements, which they would now cruelly, (I may say) ravish from them, after *they* themselves, with folded arms and indolence, have stood by a long time, and seen the others, with the greatest toil and expense, make these improvements. And the only reason that can be given for it is, they want something of *this kind*, and having none, they have made of their own ; they take this as the shortest way of obtaining it. For to this day these proprietors of Bow have not settled five families within their whole township ; and there is a great part of it clear of any dispute, and that part too which is nearest to the settlements within, yet nothing is done there, but they must needs overlook that, to come at this, the mark at which their whole view was directed. In short, they have not in the run of twenty years done as much towards settling a plantation, as they might, and as the others did, in two years ; yet they are so partial to themselves, so blinded by interest, as to think, that because they once run a line round this land, &c. above twenty years ago, they have an indefeasible right to it, which yet they are unwilling to have brought to the test, and decided fairly in the cheapest way, but endeavor, by piece meal, to destroy the possessors. In fine, it seems they have set their eyes and hearts upon this vineyard, and *perfas aut nefas* they must have it ; for the actions they have recovered (which are several) have been against common right, the common known principles of law, and plain common sense. So much do they find their account in, and means to obtain juries, entire strangers to these things, or under the influence of a principle worse than ignorance.

But the plaintiffs object to the defendant's title several matters. That which they pretend to be very material is first— The land called Rumford lies not within the bounds of what is now the province of the Massachusetts Bay, according to the last settlement of the line, the defendant himself will own ; and that settlement was not a new boundary now first made, but is to be considered in this view, viz. A declaration of his Majesty, of what was always the true boundaries of these provinces, that the province of New-Hampshire was always supposed to join to the Massachusetts, wherever the dividing lines should be fixed, and the lands now under consideration, lying in New-Hampshire, the government of the Massachusetts had no jurisdiction, or, which amounts to the same, if these lands were out of their jurisdiction, (" and the right of granting of lands was limited to the right of jurisdiction") their grant was void *ab initio ;* and therefore the settlers under them could derive no title to them-

13

selves, but must be looked upon as, or actually were, disseisors. But as their entry was recent when Bow was granted, the proprietors might lawfully enter upon them ; especially considering the government of New-Hampshire had forewarned and forbid the committee, who were on the business of beginning the settlement of Pennicoke, to proceed in the name of the government of New-Hampshire. So there was really nothing in the way of the proprietors of Bow, any more than if there had been nobody there.

Before notice is taken of the principal objection, it cannot escape the most superficial observer, how weak it is for the plaintiffs to lay stress on this forewarning, by order of the government of New-Hampshire, and in the next breath, as it were, to confess, that the government had nothing to do with it ; that the land was private property to which this related, an hundred years before. But as to the grand objection the defendant replies—When the land was appropriated as aforesaid for a township, the government of the Massachusetts had the jurisdiction in fact. Suppose it not to be *de jure*, to whom were they answerable for mal-administration ? not to the proprietors of Bow, nor even the government of New-Hampshire, for that government, by the commission then in force, did not reach to the place now under consideration, by several miles, as was hinted before ; then they could have nothing to do or say in the case. Who then was to correct this usurpation ? The King was so far from charging them with any imputation of that kind, that he approved and confirmed the act by which the inhabitants of this plantation were incorporated ; and as to the proprietors of Mason's right, they were glad they had such good neighbors, for every acre these inhabitants cultivated, doubled the value of as many acres of those proprietors. Moreover, the government of the Massachusetts exercised all the powers and authorities of government, both legislative and executive, over all places, to the line three miles northward of Merrimack aforesaid, till the said last settlement, which were never annulled, or declared to be void, as must have been the case, had this notion been entertained, which these plaintiffs advance, that the said settlement of the line was only a declaration of what was always the true boundaries of these provinces ; or that *all* which the Massachusetts had done in this regard, was a mere nullity. And if the King has not seen it proper to nullify all those acts of government, what have the plaintiffs to do in the case ? It seems necessary that all should be deemed valid, or all void ; or by what rule can a distinction be fixed ? Besides, the settlement of this line, was only to settle the jurisdiction, and not to affect private property ; nor was it ever designed to furnish a rule whereby *that* should be determined. And the acts done by either government within their respective limits, as exercised and used before the settlement, must be held valid to all intents, to avoid that confusion which the contrary notion would necessarily introduce, and which arises from connecting ideas which have no necessary connexion. That is, that the rights of government and the rights of property are always united, or that the latter has a necessary dependance on the former ; which, with respect to this very line, has in fact stirred a multitude of suits. If this opinion was true, the jurisdiction of a government ought never to be altered, without first hearing all parties whose properties would be thereby affected, which must be all those who have any real estates between the old and new line. And in what case of this nature was this ever done ? And yet if settled without it, that is without hearing such parties and determining their respective rights, this position would, in case of such alteration, (which frequently happens) be productive of the greatest mischief to private persons, not only by exposing them to suits, but by the ruin of those who held under the government whose jurisdiction should be contracted. Suppose the alteration in this case (as it might) had been, by fixing the line ten or twenty miles further eastwards, would the notion that such a settlement was only a declaration of what was always, &c. then have prevailed ? and that all the real estates lying westward of the line must belong to the inhabitants of the Massachusetts, and the old possessors be sent a grazing, or to look out and subdue new lands, and perhaps by that time they should be well settled, the like event might happen. Besides, where shall we stop ? Many or most of the ancient inhabitants within the towns of the same government, have derived their estates from town grants, which are laid out on any of the commons not before laid out in severalty, or appropriated. And by this rule, upon an alteration of the bounds of any two towns contiguous, there must arise the like transmutation of property and endless controversies ; for these towns are to many purposes distinct governments, and the governments are only larger corporations. Now the cases here put are the same in kind, and differ only in degree. From all which considerations, and many more that might be added, it follows, that the grants made by the government of the Massachusetts, before the settlement of the said line, within the jurisdiction they then had in fact, as well as other acts of government, must be held good, and the grant under which the defendant holds among the rest. Besides all this, with respect to the property of the soil, there is another matter to be considered. It appears by the present charter of the Massachusetts, that the property of the soil from forty to forty-eight degrees of north latitude, was granted to the council of Plymouth, and is a fact so well known, it is needless to offer evidence of it. It also appears by the recital in said charter, that the said council by their deed, dated the 19th of March, the third of Charles I. granted to Sir Henry Roswell, and others there named, their heirs and assigns, and their associates forever, all that part of New-England, &c. comprehending the whole tract of land, which was called the Colony of the Massachusetts Bay, under the old charter. That about a year after, King Charles confirmed this grant by a double recital, first by referring to the deed made by the council, and then by the particular bounds in that deed, and made the grantees and others their associates, a corporation on the place. That many years after this, in the latter part of the reign of King Charles II. this corporation was dissolved, by vacating the letters patent of King Charles I.

Now from these facts it may be observed, that the council of Plymouth, having the fee, conveyed the same, of all the land within the bounds of their deed of the 19th of March aforesaid, to Sir Henry Roswell, &c. as private persons, it being made a year before the corporation had existence, and had no relation to any corporate capacity. That the confirmation of the Crown aforesaid admits that the grantees of the council had the fee of the soil, which is the thing they designed to convey, and if it had not been done, there was nothing for the confirmation to work upon, for a confirmation of a void conveyance is also void. That the judgment, by which the corporation was dissolved, relates wholly to the King's letters patent, by which the corporation was erected, and has no manner of reference to the deed made by the council of Plymouth. The quere here is then upon annulling the charter of incorporation, what became of the fee of the land purchased by some of the members of that corporation as private persons, before the corporation was in esse ; or how could the vacating or destroying a particular political relation, an *ens rationis* any ways affect the right of property ? If it is said, that the said judgment nullified those letters patent as a deed of confirmation : Suppose it—but what follows ? Nothing as to this point. For the rule is, a confirmation is to bind the right of him who makes it, but not to alter the nature of the estate of him to whom made. Now if the grantees in the first deed had the fee by that, the confirmation, when in force, did not alter the nature of their estate, nor when annihilated, (if it could be so in that respect) did that affect it. Upon the whole, as to this point, it is submitted whether the dissolution of the corporation affected the right of property any more than it did the moral state of those who were the particular members. The consequence of all is, the right and property of all the lands within the bounds of that deed, was in those grantees, and still is in those who hold under them. How far those bounds extended, the judgment of the King in council, according to the opinion of the Lords Chief Justices upon the complaint of Mason and Gorges, in the year 1677, is an irrefragable determination. That as to that part of the bounds which relates to the lands of Rumford, it was to run parallel to the river at the distance of three miles northwardly of it to the head, or as it is in the report, to the *utmost extent* of the river, &c. ; whereby it run a long ways beyond the said township of Rumford, so that there can be no doubt whether it took in those lands. Now, supposing this right to remain still in private hands, what have the government of New-

Hampshire, or Mason either, to do with it? And here again the application of the rule above referred to offers itself. The land is neither the plaintiffs' nor defendant's. How then shall the plaintiffs recover? Not by the known established rules of law, but by a new method; the land the plaintiffs demand is not the defendant's, therefore *they* will have it. But here a question arises. Supposing all to be true with respect to this right that has been alleged, which way did it ever come to be the government's again? And if the property still remains in private persons, what have the government to do to parcel it out, and put whom they please in possession? There is no doubt but the re-incorporation restored the government to all they had before, not expressly excepted in the new charter; and as they had the King's confirmation as a corporation, while that capacity continued, they must be supposed to hold by that; but when that was annulled, they were remitted to their ancient right, which they had before the corporation was created. And it is submitted, whether by necessary operation of law, a corporation dissolved, and afterwards incorporated by a new charter, either by the same or a new name, is not of course restored to all its old rights and privileges, without express words in the new charter for that purpose; and if it is, the question is answered. However the government has been in possession of, and has exercised the right of granting the lands to the inhabitants more than sixty years, and if any particular person or persons might once have claimed it, such right seems to be extinguished by non-claiming the possession or exercise aforesaid. The deed made by the council of Plymouth is not in the case, nor is it to be found, nor any record of it, only by way of recital, it being probably consumed, and the record of it, with many other papers of a public nature, by the violence of a fire that destroyed the state-house, with a great part of the town of Boston, in the year 1711. But by the recital in the charter it may be depended upon as undoubted fact, that there was such a deed.

There is another objection made by the plaintiffs to the defendant's title, which is, that the committee appointed by the General Court to have the care of settling these lands at Pennicoke, were to execute deeds to the settlers, which does not appear to have been done, therefore they have no title.

The answer to which is, there was no need of it, for the land was designed for those who would settle there; the committee determined who they should be, took a list of their names, then the lots severed were drawn in their names, and set off to them; and by the terms proposed, if they perfected the settlement, the land was to be theirs. And by the act or law of the province, by which they were incorporated, past the seventh of his Majesty's reign, it appears that they had fully complied with the terms the General Court had fixed. So that the executing such deeds, as it would have been a considerable trouble and charge, so it would have been *ex abundanti*, and was therefore omitted. The

government conceded, the settlers had *their right*, and the committee could have given no more ; and as to the method of conveyance, it is immaterial. Nor was it ever customary to pass
deeds in these cases ; and was mentioned rather to stimulate the
settlers to comply with the terms, that they might be entitled to
the land, than a thing necessary to be done.—And now to sum
up all in a few words.

The defendant has entered, subdued, and cultivated the lands
demanded ; reduced them from the rough condition in which
nature left them, to the state of a garden, in which labor he has
spent more than twenty years, while the plaintiffs have been
looking on, neither asserted their claim, nor attempted to settle
any other part of their lands. And whether the defendant has
any title or not, the plaintiffs ought not to recover, if they do
not make out the title they set up. For *melior est conditio pos-
sidentis*, the government of New-Hampshire did not extend to
the place where these lands lay on the westerly side of Merrimack river, and therefore no right could be derived from
them ; and if the government had reached so far, the Crown had
long before divested itself of all right to the soil, which was
afterwards vested in Sir Henry Roswell, &c. That if that was
not the case, it was Mr. Mason's, or those who have his right ;
from whom the plaintiffs have derived no title, because the defendant was in possession at the time of making the deed and
release aforesaid. That if the release operates as to these lands,
it is in favor of the defendant. That the defendant has a good
right under the government of the Massachusetts Bay, as they
had the jurisdiction in fact, and moreover had the right of the
soil by the deed and other matters aforesaid. Add to all that,
whoever settles land in the wilderness, and of that which before
served only as a shelter and nursery for wild beasts, and a lurking
place for the more savage animals, the Indians, not only pur-
chases it at a dear rate, and has a hard bargain, though the land
is given to him, but does public service. In which regard the
whole town of Rumford merits the thanks of the government,
instead of being turned out of doors. And what may be said in
behalf of the defendant in this case, may, with the same propriety, be urged in behalf of those other inhabitants of Rumford,
with whom these proprietors, or those who derived their right
from them, are now contending, and have actions in the courts
under continuance.

———

[The foregoing document was draw up by the late Judge Pickering, and formed one of the papers upon which the controversy
was decided in 1762. Though of considerable length, it will be
interesting to the people of Concord, who will here see the entire ground occupied by the parties fully explored. The decision
of the King in Council follows, which, though referring to other

appeals, is applicable to the whole. The dispute, however, was not completely settled, until the proprietors of Bow had extorted large sums from the inhabitants of Rumford, by way of compromise.]

At the Court of St. James, the 29th day of December, 1762.

PRESENT,

The King's Most Excellent Majesty,

Earl of Huntington,	Viscount Falmouth,
Earl of Halifax,	Mr. Vice Chamberlain,
Earl of Northumberland,	George Grenville, Esq.
Earl of Egremont,	Henry Fox, Esq.
Earl Delaware,	Welbore Ellis, Esq.

Upon reading at the Board a Report from the Right Honorable the Lords of the Committee of Council, for hearing appeals from the plantations, dated the 17th of this instant, in the words following, viz. :—

Your Majesty having been pleased, by your order in council of the 15th of February, 17—, to refer unto this committee the humble petition and appeal of Benjamin Rolfe, Esq. Daniel Carter, Timothy Simonds, John Evans, John Chandler, Abraham Colby, and Abraham Kimball, setting forth, amongst other things, that in 1721, Benjamin Stevens and others petitioned the General Court or Assembly of the Massachusetts Bay, for a grant of land at Pennicook, upon the river Merrimack, which petition, having been referred to a committee of both Houses, and they reported in favor of the application, that it would be for the advantage of the province that part of the land petitioned for should be assigned and set apart for a township, to contain seven miles square, and to begin where Contoocook river falls into Merrimack river. And they appointed a committee to bring forward the said settlement, and laid down several special directions with regard thereto. And amongst others, that the lands should be divided into one hundred and three lots or shares ; and that one hundred persons or families, able to make their settlement, should be admitted, and each settler to pay for his lot five pounds for the use of the province, and be obliged to build a good house for the family within three years, and break up and fence in a certain quantity of land, and the houses and lots to be on each side the river ; and that a meeting-house should be erected and finished, which was to be assigned for the use of the minister and for the school, and the charge of the committee was to be borne by the settlers ; which Report was agreed to by both Houses of the Council and Assembly of that province, and concurred in by the Governor. That in 1726, the town of Pennicook was laid out, and divided into lots amongst the proprietors, who began and carried on a settlement there with great difficulty and cost, it being above twenty miles up into the Indian country, beyond any English settlement then made, and being a perfect wilderness, having not the least sign that human foot had ever trod the ground there, and notwithstanding the difficulties they were under in establishing a new town in so remote a desert, they pursued their undertaking with such industry and pains, clearing the land, building houses, sowing corn, &c. that within a few years a town was erected, and the place capable of receiving their families, who were then removed up there.

That on the 6th of August, 1728, in consideration that five hundred acres of land, which had prior to the aforesaid Pennicook grant, been granted to Governor Endicott, fell within the Pennicook boundaries, the Assembly of the Massachusetts Bay came to a resolution, which was concurred in by the Governor and Council, that the Pennicook settlers should be allowed and empowered, by a surveyor and chain-men upon oath, to extend the south bounds of their township one hundred and thirty rods the breadth of their town, and the same was accordingly granted and confirmed to them as an equivalent for the said five hundred acres of land. And in a few years they had so far erected and settled a town, that in 1733, the Governor, Council, and Assembly of the Massachusetts Bay passed an act for erecting the said plantation of Pennicook into a township, by the name of Rumford; which act was confirmed by his late Majesty in council; and the said settlers having ever since, at great costs and labor, gone on improving the lands within the said township of Rumford, by building, cultivation, and otherwise ; and having been in continual possession thereof for above thirty years past, and the same is now become a frontier town on that part of New-Hampshire.

That on the 6th of August, 1728, David Melvin and William Ayer petitioned the General Court or Assembly of the Massachusetts Bay, for themselves and others, who had served as volunteers under Capt. John Lovewell, praying a part of the province land might be granted to them for a township, in consideration of the service they had done, and the great difficulties they had undergone in the war ; which petition being read in the House of Representatives, it was resolved, that six miles square of land, lying on each side of Merrimack river, of the same breadth from Merrimack river as the township of Pennicook, and to begin where Pennicook new grant determines, and from thence to extend the lines of the east and the west bounds on right angles, until the six miles square should be completed, be, and it is thereby granted to the forty-seven soldiers, and the legal representatives of such of them as were deceased, who marched with Capt. Lovewell, (himself included) when he engaged the enemy at Pigwacket. That on the 9th of July, 1729, the said David Melvin and others, petitioned the Assembly of the Massachusetts Bay, setting forth, that they had caused the said tract of land to be surveyed and platted, and praying a confirmation thereof, and that the grantees might be empowered to assemble and chose a clerk, pass votes, and be empowered to admit the persons in Capt. Lovewell's first march, to be associated with him ; and the survey or plan of the said tract, which is annexed to the petition, and mentions it to begin at the south-east corner of the said other town of Pennicook, and from thence to run out according to the grant. It was ordered, that the land described in the plan should be confirmed to the petitioners and their associates, and their heirs and assigns forever, provided it exceeded not six miles square, nor interfered with any former grant. And the Assembly, on the 23d of September following, ordered a preference to be given to those soldiers who were actually with the Captain in the engagement when he killed several of the Indians, and the said resolutions of the Assembly were concurred in by the Governor and Council.

That the Suncook proprietors carried on their said settlement which adjoined to Pennicook, otherwise Rumford, in like manner as the Pennicook or Rumford settlers had done ; and in 1737, had a minister settled there, and by their industry, labor, and charges, it became a good parish, filled with inhabitants.

That some years since, upon a dispute about the boundary line between the provinces of the Massachusetts Bay and New-Hampshire, his Majesty was pleased to issue a commission to mark out the dividing line between the said province of New-Hampshire and Massachusetts Bay, but with an express declaration, that private property should not be affected thereby. And upon hearing the Report of the commissioners appointed to settle the said boundary, his Majesty was pleased, by his order in council, made in 1740, to adjudge and order that the northern boundary of the said province of the Massachusetts Bay are and be a similar curve line, pursuing the course of Merrimack river at three miles distance on the north side thereof, beginning at the Atlantic ocean, and ending at a point due north of a place called Pautucket falls, and a strait line drawn from thence due west cross the said river, till it meets with his Majesty's other governments ; by which determination two-third parts at least of the said river Merrimack, with the lands and settlements thereon, and among the rest, the said towns of Pennicook or Rumford, and Suncook, would lay upon the said river considerably above the said Pautucket falls, were excluded out of the said province of Massachusetts Bay, in which they had before been thought and reputed to be, and thrown into the said other province of New-Hampshire. That notwithstanding his Majesty had been pleased, at the time of issuing the said commission to fix the said boundary, to declare the same was not to affect private property. Yet, certain persons in New-Hampshire, desirous to make the labors of others an advantage to themselves,

14

and to possess themselves of the towns of Pennicook, otherwise
Rumford, and Suncook, as now improved by the industry of the
appellants and the said first settlers thereof, whom they seek to
despoil of the benefit of all their labors, did, on the first of November, 1759, by the name of the proprietors of the common and
undivided lands, lying and being within the township of Bow,
brought an ejectment in the inferior court of common pleas,
holden at Portsmouth, in New-Hampshire, against the appellants,
by which ejectment the respondents, under the general denomi-
nation aforesaid of the proprietors of Bow, demand against the
appellants the possession of about one thousand acres of land,
alleging the same to lie in Bow aforesaid, and to be described
and bounded as therein mentioned and set forth in the ejectment, their grant of the town of Bow, dated the 20th of May,
1727, from John Wentworth, Esq. lieutenant-governor of New-
Hampshire ; and that by force thereof they were seized in fee
of the lands thereby granted, to the extent of eighty-one square
miles, and they had afterwards entered thereon, pursuant to
their grant, and were seized thereof, and alleged they were
entitled to the one thousand acres of land sued for, as part of the
said eighty-one miles square of land, and that the same lay within the said town of Bow ; but that the appellants had entered
therein and ejected the respondents, and withheld the same
from them.   To which action the appellants severally pleaded
not guilty, as to so much of the lands sued for as were in their
respective possessions.

That on the 2d of September, 1760, the cause was brought on
to trial in the said inferior court, when the jury gave a verdict
for the respondents, and judgment was entered up accordingly
with costs, from which the appellants prayed, and were allowed
an appeal to the next superior court. And on the 2d Tuesday in
November, 1760, the cause was brought on again to trial in the
superior court, when the jury gave their verdict for the respondents, and the judgment was thereupon entered up, affirming the
said judgment of the inferior court with costs.   That the appellants conceiving themselves to be thereby greatly aggrieved,
prayed, and were allowed an appeal therefrom to your Majesty
in council, and humbly pray, that both the said verdicts and judgments may be reversed, and that they may be otherwise reliev-
ed in the premises.

The Lords of the committee, in obedience to your Majesty's
said order of reference, this day took the said petition and appeal into their consideration, and heard all parties therein concerned, by their council, learned in the law, and do agree humbly to report as their opinion to your Majesty, that the said
judgment of the inferior court of common pleas of the province
of New-Hampshire, of the 2d of September, 1760, and also the
judgment of the superior court of judicature of the 2d Tuesday
in November, 1760, affirming the same, should be both of them
reversed, and that the appellants should be restored to what
they have lost by means of said judgments.

His Majesty this day took the said Report into consideration, and was pleased, with the advice of his privy council, to approve thereof, and to order, as it is hereby ordered, that the said judgment of the inferior court of common pleas of the province of New-Hampshire, of the 2d of September, 1760, and also the judgment of the superior court of judicature, of the 2d Tuesday in November, affirming the same, to be both of them reversed, and that the appellants be restored to what they may have lost by means of the said judgments, whereof the Governor or commander in chief of his Majesty's province of New-Hampshire, for the time being, and all others whom it may concern. are to take notice and govern themselves accordingly.

[No. VI.]

HEALTH, LONGEVITY, &C.

Synopsis of the Bills of Mortality for the town of Concord, from the year 1798 to 1822.—By THOMAS CHADBOURNE, M. D.

		Tot.
1798	25, 2w. 17ᶜ 70, 4m, 4. 2. 1. 40, 53ᶜ 38, 7ᶜ 67ᶜ 7. 4m.	
	49, 2. 0. 8. 2. 66ᶜ 0. 43,	26
1799	3. 5. 57ᶜ 81ᶜ 51ᶜ 1. 80ᶜ 8m. 8. 60ᶜ 30, 32, 10d. 21ᶜ 60,	15
1800	10w. 20ᶜ 50ᶜ 83ᶜ 78ᶜ 88ᶜ 13. 18m. 46, 8m. 18m. 2. 2.	
	4. 60ᶜ 0. 91ᶜ 7. 9. 4. 1. 0. 0.	25
1801	4d. 1d. 31, 0. 82, 21ᶜ 18m. 18m. 80ᶜ 21ᶜ 4d. 20d. 49,	
	22, 6m. 70ᶜ 45, 20ᶜ 49, 97, 2. 37, 28,	24
1802	70, 37, 56ᶜ 48, 24, 0. 73, 83, 1. 5. 2. 3. 53, 3. 3. 18m.	
	4. 2. 5. 9. 19ᶜ 82, - - - - -	22
1803	86, 80ᶜ 63, 60, 85ᶜ 2. 6. 0. 55, 65, 3. 23, 28, 4. 6. 0.	
	67ᶜ 43ᶜ 65ᶜ 0. 18m. 30ᶜ 3. 33, 80ᶜ 0. 18m. 69ᶜ 19ᶜ 2.	
	29ᶜ 0. 0. 0. 0. 53ᶜ	36
1804	70ᶜ 40ᶜ 3. 19ᶜ 0. 0. 72ᶜ 1. 0. 65ᶜ 53, 68ᶜ 2. 65ᶜ 25, 1.	
	1. 89ᶜ 2. 1. 45ᶜ 88, 0. 0. - - - - -	23
1805	71, 50, 36ᶜ 68ᶜ 0. 0. 22, 0. 90, 64ᶜ 0. 20, 1. 8. 45, 22ᶜ	
	22ᶜ 1. 45ᶜ 10. 64ᶜ 0. 67, 57, 10. 0. 92, - -	27
1806	79ᶜ 2. 66ᶜ 0. 0. 0. 59ᶜ 22, 32ᶜ 24, 57, 92, 63, -	13
1807	18, 76ᶜ 0. 18, 60ᶜ 20, 0. 66, 84ᶜ 70ᶜ 0. 35ᶜ 0. 10. 86ᶜ	
	0. 0. 83, 5. 14, 28, 3. - - - - -	22
1808	0. 0. 80ᶜ 2. 16, 58, 53, 35, 20, 17, 0. 18m. 27ᶜ 5. 40,	
	0. 50ᶜ 45ᶜ 95ᶜ - - - - - -	19
1809	80ᶜ 2. 8. 0. 0. 0. 82, 29ᶜ 4. 70ᶜ 71, 22, 2. 27, 2. 1. 0.	
	0. 41, 30, 65,	21
1810	9ᶜ 65, 33, 45ᶜ 2. 14, 31, 92ᶜ 32ᶜ 0. 22, 17, 65, 63ᶜ	14
1811	41ᶜ 82, 1. 11. 4. 74ᶜ 86, 19, 0. 32ᶜ 74ᶜ 31ᶜ 27ᶜ 64ᶜ 74ᶜ	
	5. 0. 37ᶜ 70ᶜ 3. 31, 25, 0. 46ᶜ 0. 3. 0. 0. 32ᶜ 0. 70, 3.	
	25ᶜ 59, 50ᶜ 0. 47, 73, 82ᶜ 11, 33, - - -	41
	From December 1811, to January 1819, inclusive, there were 250 deaths—there is no record of the ages to be found.	250

Total, 578

Diseases and Casualties during the years 1819, 1820, 1821 *and*
1822.

Angina Maligna	7' - - - -	1
Consumption	40, 27, 22' 37, 28, 51' 40' 32, 29' 51, 16,	
	34, 25, 28' 15' months, 30, 28, 46' 30.	
	19' 30, 28, 30, 23, - - -	24
Cancer	84' 65, - - - - -	2
Apoplexy	54' - - - - - -	1
Infantile Fever	18m' 6w' 6m' 12w' 8w' 3y. 18m,	7
Fits	59' 2' 6d' - - - -	3
Inflammation of } the Brain	19, 27' - - - -	2
Spina Bifida	6w' - - - - -	1
Scrophula	16' 51, - - - - -	2
Dropsy	52' 74' 1' 46, 30' 71, 3' 10' -	8
Old Age	68, 78, 80' 91, 86' 69, 73' 81' 85, 96,	38
	78, 88' 70, 81' 85, 80' 77, 75' 96' 82'	
	78' 85' 72, 85' 99' 76' 70- 86' 77, 73'	
	76' 30, 70, - - - -	
Petechia sine } Febri	30' - - - - - -	1
Drowned	20' 35' - - - - -	2
Fever Pulmonia	20, 30' 69' - - - -	3
" Typhus	26' 18' 18' 35' 66' 30' 47' 25, 68' 40' 32'	11
" Puerperal	40, 30, 27' - - - -	3
Infantile disea- } ses	1' 3w' 2d' 6w' 3d' 6w' 2d' 1y' 4m' 1m' 2n' 2' 3. - - - -	13
Quinsey	1' 8' 7' 2' 6d' - - - -	5
Delirium tremens	49' 27' - - - - -	2
Intemperance	40' 60' 51' - - - -	3
Scalded	3' - - - - - -	1
Abdominal In- } flammation	55' 50, 19, 17' - - -	4
Dysenteria	20m' - - - - -	1
Sudden	73' 43' - - - - -	2
Unknown	51' 2' 32' 0, 0, 2' 17' 8' 0, 0' 28, -	11

Total   150

It is ascertained that from Jan. 1792, to Dec. 1797, there were
117 deaths, which makes the whole number of deaths during the
last thirty years, 803.

The above table is correct as to the number of deaths, but is
very imperfect in other respects. In many instances in the record of infants, there is no distinction of the sex, and in some
cases, the *age* of infants is not inserted. Such are distinguished by
a *cypher* thus, 0. A *comma* after the age denotes the females, and
the *inverted comma* the male sex. Those cases where no record
of sex was made are distinguished by a *point.*

From the above abstract of the diseases and deaths, for the last thirty years, it is reasonable to infer that the inhabitants enjoy an unusual exemption from disease. Scarcely any infectious disease has ever been known in this town ; and very few cases of consumption, in comparison with other low situated places, occur here. Each morning in the summer season the land contiguous to the river is covered with a thick fog : this fog in frosty seasons prevents the destruction of vegetables ; and is supposed to cleanse the air of impurities, which are swept to the ocean by the current of the Merrimack.

About the commencement, and during the war of the revolution, the Small Pox often appeared in different sections of the country, owing, probably, to the frequent communications with Canada, where the disease then prevailed ; to the free intercourse that was necessarily held by the people with the soldiers and army, and in some instances it was supposed to have been sent into the country as a means of annoyance by the enemy.

In July, 1775, Dr. Carrigain visited a patient in a neighboring town, who proved to be sick with the Small Pox. He took it the natural way. The nature of his disease was not discovered, until John, the son of Mr. Nathaniel West, who lived on the opposite side of the street from Dr. C. also took the disease. The Doctor inoculated his own family, then consisting of five members, who all recovered. Mr. West's family consisted of nine, six of whom had the disease the natural way, the others escaped. Mr. West, aged 58, died. It was first known on Saturday that the Small Pox was in the town ; so great was the alarm, that the next morning (Sunday) the inhabitants assembled, en masse, and commenced the erection of a " Pest House" in a retired grove west of the late residence of Capt. Benjamin Emery, and such was the zeal and activity with which they applied themselves to the work, that by night a convenient house to consist of four rooms had been hewed, framed, and raised, and the boards for covering, and brick for the chimney were drawn on to the ground. Dr. Carrigain and his family remained at their own house opposite to where Charles Walker, Esq. now resides ; fences were run across the street to cut off all communication, and a road was opened through the fields. Mr. West's family was conveyed to the Pest House. None of the inhabitants were inoculated. The house afterwards served occasionally for the reception of transient soldiers of the army, who either had or were suspected to have the disease.

The question naturally arises, why were not all who were exposed to the infection immediately inoculated ? A law was then in force " for the prevention of the spread of the Small Pox," which forbid under a penalty any person inoculating without leave from court, and the people in those days were brought up in the belief that laws were made to be obeyed.

In 1793, the Small Pox again appeared in a family in the westerly part of the town. The family consisted of thirteen mem-

bers, all of whom had the disease without inoculation. Mr.
Jonathan Stickney, the father, and an infant child, died. The
manner in which the infection was conveyed to this family never
has with certainty been ascertained.

In the winter of 1812–13, when the disease known by the different appellations of *Malignant Pleurisy, Spotted Fever, Bilious
Pneumonia,* &c. spread so generally through the N. E. States,
this town was visited in common with others. The character of
the disease was that of a *Typhoid Pneumonia,* not alarming at
first, but in its progress discovering a malignancy that too often
rendered ineffectual all the boasted remedies of our profession.
It was, however, confined principally to the soldiery, then quar-
tered in the town—but few of the citizens fell victims to it.*

In the winter of 1816–17, the disease appeared again in the
westerly section of the town, preceded by a season, remarkable
for its coldness, long droughts and frequent frosts, that almost destroyed the hopes of the husbandman. It now assumed a character different from its appearance in other places. Its accession
in the worst cases was by an erysipelatous inflammation of the ex-
tremities, that soon ran into gangrene, and generally destroyed
the patient.

The summer of 1816 was uncommonly cold throughout the
United States, and throughout Europe, except some of the most
northern parts of it. Vegetation was very materially affected
by this state of the weather. The small grains generally were
in abundance, and very good, but the crops of hay were deficient,
and Indian corn, by the frosts in August, was almost lost. But for
the inclemency of the season, the inhabitants were compensated
with a greater share of health than had ever been known since
the settlement of the town.

Those who are in the habit of noting the effects of the varia-
tions of the weather on the human constitution will recollect that
hot and dry summers are uniformly unhealthy—*hot and wet* sum
mers *less* so.—This season, which was *cold and dry* was the most
healthy throughout the United States of any 'in the recollection
of the oldest physicians.

The number of inhabitants in this town in 1767, was 752;
1052 in 1775; 1747 in 1790; 2052 in 1800; 2393 in 1810;
2838 in 1820. The average number of deaths for the last thirty
years has been 27. Of the whole number of deaths about one
12th part have lived to the age of 80 years and upwards—several to nearly 100. The names of 85 aged persons, are found a-
mong the records of deaths kept since 1798, whose ages amount
to 6634 years. In the year 1815, there were living in this town
60 persons, whose ages amounted to the sum of 4320 years.

---

* The Spotted Fever, in 1813, made its appearance March 10, and continued until the middle of May.

Cases of the inhabitants,				98	deaths	6
Regular Soldiers,		.	.	49	"	7
Volunteers,	.	.	.	100	"	11
				247		24

[NO. VII.]

Names of the Physicians, Attorneys and Justices of the Peace who have resided in Concord.

PHYSICIANS.

1. Dr. Ezra Carter, from South-Hampton, settled here in 1740 ; died in 1767.—*See page* 35.

2. Dr. ——— Emery, who afterwards settled and died at Frye-burgh, Me.

3. Dr. Ebenezer H. Goss, son of the Rev. Thomas Goss, of Bolton, Mass. He married a daughter of Rev. Mr. Walker, and now resides in Paris, Maine.

4. Dr. Philip Carrigain, born in New-York, settled here in 1768, and died in 1806.—*See page* 62.

5. Dr. Peter Green, A. M., M. M. S. Hon. Soc. was born at Lancaster, Mass. in 1745 ; graduated at Harvard Coll. 1766 ; removed to Concord in 1772, and has practised successfully more than half a century.

6. Dr. Samuel Adams, M. D. from Lincoln, Ms. practised here a short time.

7. Dr. Zadok Howe, M. D. from Franklin, Ms. practised here several years ; removed to Billerica, in 1814.

8. Dr. Thomas Chadbourne, M. D. commenced practice here in 1814 ; and is one of the present physicians.

9. Dr. Moses Long, from Hopkinton, practised in this town several years, and removed in 1823.

10. Dr. Moses Chandler settled here in 1816, and is a practising physician.

11. Dr. Henry Bond, M. D. practised a few years, and removed to Philadelphia, in 1820.

12. Dr. Samuel Morril, from Epsom, removed into this town in 1820 ; and is in practice.

13. Dr. Peter Renton, from Scotland, settled in this place in 1822, and is in practice.

ATTORNEYS AT LAW.

*Peter Green,
*Edward St. Loe Livermore,
†Samuel Green,
Charles Walker, H. 1793.
‖Philip Carrigain, D. 1794.
*Thomas W. Thompson, H. 1786.
Moody Kent, H. 1801.

§*William Pickering*, H. 1797.
Samuel A. Kimball, D. 1806.
Samuel Fletcher, D. 1810.
George Kent, D. 1814.
Richard Bartlett, D. 1815.
Amos A. Parker, D. 1819.

*Deceased. †Now Associate Justice of the Superior Court. ‖Removed to Chichester. §State Treasurer.

JUSTICES OF THE PEACE,

In Concord, since the adoption of the constitution in 1784, with the date of their appointments.

*Peter Green, * ‖ Dec. 25, 1784.
*Timothy Walker, * ‖ Dec. 25, 1784.

*Aaron Kinsman, Jan. 4, 1787.
*William Duncan, May 16, 1791.
John Bradley, May 16, 1791.
William A. Kent, * || June 13, 1796.
*Thomas W. Thompson, * Dec. 1, 1796. (1)
*Jacob Abbot,** June 20, 1797. (2)
Samuel Green, * || Dec. 6, 1800.
Stephen Ambrose, * Dec. 8, 1800.
Jonathan Wilkins, June 19, 1802.
Albe Cady, * June 19, 1802. (3)
Philip Carrigain, * June 12, 1805.
Isaac Emery, Dec. 12, 1808.
*Peter C. Farnum, Dec. 13. 1808.
Timothy Carter, Dec. 13, 1808.
Samuel Morril, Dec. 12, 1808. (4)
Charles Walker, * June 15, 1805.
Ballard Haseltine, May 31, 1809.
Jonathan Eastman, Sept. 20, 1810.
William Pickering, Sept. 20. 1810. (5)
Samuel Sparhawk, * May 30, 1811.
*Paul Rolfe, June 15, 1812.
John Odlin, June 18, 1813.
Samuel A. Kimball, Sept. 17, 1813.(6)
Moody Kent, * Jan. 31, 1814.
Isaac Hill, Nov. 5, 1819.
Amos A. Parker, 1819.
Isaac Dow, June 22, 1821.
Richard Bradley, June 28, 1821.
Jonathan Eastman, Jr. do.
Samuel Fletcher, June 29, 1821.
Richard Bartlett　　do.　　1821.
George Kent,　　do.　　1821.
John Farmer, May 16, 1823.
Robert Davis, Nov. 1823.

(1) Then residing in Salisbury.—(2) Now of Brunswick, Me.—(3) Then residing in Plainfield.—(4) Then of Epsom.—(5) Then of Greenland —(6)Then of Dover.

Those *preceded* by a * are dead ; those in *Italicks* are not in commission ; those *followed* by a * were afterwards *Justices of the Peace and Quorum,* and those with a || were *Justices throughout the State.*

————

[NO. VIII.]

Names of Town-Clerks,Selectmen and Representatives, since the year
1732.

TOWN CLERKS.

1732　Benjamin Rolfe, Jan. to March.	1766—1769　Benjamin Rolfe.
———　Timothy Clement, from March.	1769—1778　Timothy Walker, jr.
1733—1745　Benjamin Rolfe.	1778—1787　John Kimball.
1746—1749　Ezra Carter.	1787—1796　Caleb Chase.
1749 to 1766　Interregnum—no town offi-	1796—1819　John Odlin.
cers.	1819 to　　*Francis N. Fisk.*

SELECTMEN.

1732.—*Jan.* to *March*, Ebenezer Eastman, John Merrill, Edward Abbot.
1732.—*March.* Ebenezer Eastman, John Chandler, Jeremiah Stickney, Joseph Eastman. Edward Abbot.
1733.—Ebenezer Eastman, Benjamin Rolfe, Ephraim Farnum.
1734.—Benjamin Rolfe, Jeremiah Stickney, John Merrill.
1735.—Benjamin Rolfe, Ebenezer Eastman, Jeremiah Stickney.
1736.—Benjamin Rolfe, James Osgood, Joseph Hall.
1737.—Benjamin Rolfe, John Chandler, Richard Hazeltine.
1738—1739.—Ebenezer Eastman, Benjamin Rolfe, Barachias Farnum.
1740—1741.—Benjamin Rolfe, John Chandler, Ebenezer Eastman.
1742—1743.—Benjamin Rolfe, Ebenezer Eastman, Jeremiah Stickney.
1744—Benjamin Rolfe, Barachias Farnum, John Chandler.
1745.—Benjamin Rolfe, John Chandler, Jeremiah Stickney.
1746.—John Chandler, Ebenezer Eastman, Richard Hazeltine.
1747—1748.—Ezra Carter,John Chandler, Richard Hazeltine.
1749—John Chandler, Ezra Carter, Jeremiah Stickney, Ebenezer Virgin, Henry Lovejoy.
[From 1749 to 1766, there were no town officers appointed.]
1766—Benjamin Rolfe, Joseph Farnum, John Chandler, jr.
1767.—Richard Hazeltine, Philip Eastman, Amos Abbot.
1768.—Benjamin Rolfe, Ebenezer Hail, Reuben Kimball.
1769.—Reuben Kimball, Ebenezer Hall, Timothy Walker, jr.
1770.—Timothy Walker, jr. Reuben Kimball, Benjamin Emery.
1771.—Philip Eastman, Timothy Walker, jr. Benjamin Emery.
1772.—Timothy Walker, jr. Joseph Hall, jr. Phinehas Virgin.
1773.—John Kimball, Amos Abbot, Timothy Walker,jr.
1774.—Timothy Walker, jr. Reuben Kimball, Thomas Stickney.
1775.—Timothy Walker, jr. Reuben Kimball, Benjamin Emery.
1776-1777.—Reuben Kimball, Amos Abbot, John Kimball.
1778.—John Kimball, Joshua Abbot, Joseph Hall.
1779.—Timothy Walker, Ezekiel Dimond, John Kimball.
1780.—John Chandler, James Walker, Thomas Wilson.
1781.—Timothy Walker, John Kimball, James Walker.
1782.—Timothy Walker, Benjamin Emery, Thomas Wilson.
1783-1786.—Timothy Walker, Reuben Kimball, Thomas Stickney.
1787.—Joseph Hall, Henry Martin, Thomas Wilson.
1788.—Timothy Walker, Benjamin Emery, Chandler Lovejoy.
1789-1790.—Reuben Kimball, Timothy Walker, Asa Herrick.
1791-1793.—Timothy Walker, Reuben Kimball, Benjamin Emery.
1794.—Timothy Walker, Reuben Kimball, John Bradley.
1795-1796.—Timothy Walker, John Bradley, Henry Martin.
1797-1798.—John Odlin, Richard Ayer, John Eastman.
1799.—Timothy Walker, John Odlin, Henry Martin.
1800.—John Odlin, Jonathan Wilkins, Henry Martin.
1801.—Jonathan Wilkins, John West, Stephen Ambrose.
1802.—Timothy Walker, John West, Stephen Ambrose.
1803.—Jonathan Wilkins, John West, Stephen Ambrose.
1804-1805.—Jonathan Wilkins, John West, Amos Abbot, jr.
1806-1807.—Ebenezer Dustin, Enoch, Coffin, Edmund Leavitt.
1808.—Enoch Coffin, Samuel Butters, Timothy Carter.
1809.—John Odlin, Amos Abbot,jr. Nathaniel Abbot.
1810.—Nathaniel Abbot, Edmund Leavitt, Sherburne Wiggin.
1811.—Nathaniel Abbot, Edmund Leavitt, Abiel Walker.
1812.—Nathaniel Abbot, Amos Abbot, jr. Abiel Walker.
1813.—Nathaniel Abbot, John Odlin, Amos Abbot.
1814.—Nathaniel Abbot, Nathaniel Ambrose, Nathan Stickney.
1815.—Nathaniel Ambrose, Joshua Abbot, Richard Bradley.
1816-1817.—Joshua Abbot, Richard Bradley, Samuel Runnels.
1818.—John Odlin, Nathaniel Abbot, Nathaniel Ambrose.
1819.—Abiel Walker, Joseph Walker, Jeremiah Pecker.
1820.—Richard Bradley, Isaac Farnum, Jeremiah Pecker.
1821.—Richard Bradley, Isaac Farnum, Jeremiah Pecker.
1822.—Albe Cady, Isaac Farnum, Isaac Dow.
1822 —Jeremiah Pecker, Isaac Farnum, Isaac Dow.

REPRESENTATIVES.

1775. *May* 11.—Timothy Walker, jr. elected delegate to the provincial congress. [He was one of the committee who in 1776, drew up a declaration of Independence by this State.]
1777. Gordon Hutchins. [Col. H. being absent this year in the army, Col. Thomas Stickney was appointed.]
1778. Timothy Walker, jun.
1779. Nathaniel Rolfe.—Jonathan Hale and Timothy Walker, jr. delegates to convention in Sept.—Thomas Stickney delegate in December.
1780. Jonathan Hale.
1781. *April.* Timothy Walker, delegate to convention for forming constitution.
1782—1784. Timothy Walker.
1785. Peter Green.
1786, 7. John Bradley.
1788. Peter Green.—Benjamin Emery, delegate to convention for adoption of constitution.
1789. Peter Green.
1790. John Bradley.
1791. Timothy Walker.
1792. John Bradley.
1793. William Duncan.
1794, 5. Daniel Livermore.
1796. John Bradley.
1797. William A. Kent.
1798—1800. Jacob Abbot.
1801. William A. Kent.
1802. John Bradley.
1803—1805. William A. Kent.
1806—1808. Samuel Green.
1809, 10. Stephen Ambrose.
1811—1813. Stephen Ambrose and Thomas W. Thompson.
1814. Thomas W. Thompson and Richard Ayer.
1815. Richard Ayer and George Hough.
1816. George Hough and John Odlin.
1817. John Odlin and William A. Kent.
1818. William A. Kent and Thomas W. Thompson.
1819. Abiel Walker and Nathan Ballard, jr.
1820, 1. Stephen Ambrose and Nathaniel Abbot.
1822. Stephen Ambrose and Samuel Morril.
1823. Stephen Ambrose and Samuel Fletcher.

—··⊕●⊕··—

[NO. IX.]

MISCELLANEOUS ARTICLES.

Garrisons in 1746.

1. On the E. side the river, at Capt. Eastman's.
2. At Rev. Mr. Walker's, near Horse-shoe pond.
3. At Capt. Lovejoy's, where L. Hutchins now lives.
4. At Mr. Edward Abbot's, where the Souther house stands. [In this ancient building, now owned by Porter Blanchard, the first male and female children were born, viz. Edward and Dorcas Abbot.]
5. At Capt. Stickney's.
6. At James Osgood's—near the site of Bullard & Waterman's store.
7. At Capt. Timothy Walker's.
8. At Deac. Joseph Hall's—the Wilkins place.
9. At Jonathan Eastman's, on the mill-road.

10. There was subsequently a garrison at Deac. Abbot's, near the late residence of Mr. Thompson.

It is said, these were the only garrisons, or fortified houses, erected in this town during the Indian wars.

Newspapers published in Concord.

The first newspaper published in this town was the *Courier of New-Hampshire*, commenced by George Hough, Jan. 6, 1790; and discontinued Oct. 30, 1805.

2. *The Mirror*, by Moses Davis, was commenced Sept. 6, 1792; and discontinued in 1799.

3. *The New Star*, by Russell and Davis, was commenced in April, 1797. It was published in an octavo form weekly about six months.

4. The *Republican Gazette*, by Elijah Russell, was commenced Feb. 5, 1801; and discontinued in 1802. [Mr. Russell died at Washington, Vt. May 25, 1803.]

5. The *Concord Gazette*, by William Hoit,jr. and Jesse C. Tuttle,was commenced July 6, 1806; and its publication continued until 1819—during which time several changes took place in its proprietors.

6. The *American Patriot* was commenced Oct. 18, 1808, by William Hoit, Jr. and published until April, 1809; when Isaac Hill purchased the establishment, and altered the name of the paper to the *New-Hampshire Patriot*. It was published from 1811 to 1814, by Isaac and Walter R. Hill; and from 1819 to 1823, by Isaac Hill & Jacob B. Moore. It is now published by Isaac Hill, under the name of *New-Hampshire Patriot and State Gazette*.

7. The *Concord Observer*, by George Hough, was commenced Jan. 1, 1819, and continued to April 1, 1822; when John W. Shepard purchased the establishment, and the paper is now published by him under the name of *New-Hampshire Repository*.

8. The *New-Hampshire Statesman* was commenced by Luther Roby, Jan. 6, 1823; and is still published by him for Amos A. Parker, the editor and proprietor.

Concord Musical Society.

In 1801, Deac. Joseph Hall, "from a desire to encourage and promote the prac. tice of sacred musick in Concord," made a donation to this Society, which had been previously incorporated,* of $500 in the U. S. six per cent. stock. The orig- inal sum was to be kept entire, and the interest accruing to be applied to the benefit of said society, in such manner as a majority shall direct.

Incorporated June 15, 1799.

Notes on the Weather, &c.

[No regular journal of the weather has ever been kept by any person in Concord, and it is impossible therefore to give an accurate account of the extremes of heat and cold. The following notices are copied from a blank leaf in an old account book belonging to Mr. BENJAMIN KIMBALL, who lives near the river on the eastern shore.]

1762. The winter of this year was very severe. Snows were frequent, and so deep as to prevent passing in any direction for two months—being nearly 6 feet on the level.

1772. In January, occurred a great flood. Thick masses of ice passed down the river and were left upon the intervals.

1789. Uncommonly pleasant winter—grain sowed in December—and boating continued until 29th Jan. 1790.

1795. Boating across the river 17th January.

1796. The last boating 30th November.

1797. Nov. 25, passing on the ice.

1798. First boating April 2.

1799. First boating April 6. Spring very backward—May scarcely exhibiting the usual mildness of April.

1800. First boating April 3 ; last boating Dec. 10, and immediate passing on the ice.

1801. First boating March 12.

1802. April 4, good passing on the ice with horses.

1804. First boating April 7.

1805. Ditto March 7.

1810. Considerable frost July 18.

1812. April 13, snow fell to the depth of 6 inches. May 4th and 5th, cold snow storm. June 5, appletrees in full bloom.

1815. Snow fell first week in December, and it continued good sleighing until March following, without rain. Sept. 23d of this year will long be remembered for the violence of a gale, which extended over the whole of New-England, and was very destructive.

1816. Cold season—the hopes of the farmer cut off.

1817. First passing on the ice with horses, Dec. 23.

1818. March 1, commenced a heavy fall of rain, and on the 3d, the water rose above the banks of the river.

1819. Mild winter—journeying with wagons, &c. the whole season.'

—— April 5, great fresh, and Federal Bridge swept away by the ice.

—— May 19, extraordinary high fresh, the intervals entirely flooded, and looking like an inland sea.

1820. May 26, apple-trees in bloom—a cold storm of hail and rain—hail two inches deep.

—— Oct. 17, the highest fresh for 36 years.

1824. Feb. 10 and 11, great thaw and rain. On the 12th the river suddenly rose about 15 feet, the ice being very thick, and swept away the Federal and Concord Bridges, in part. The ice in immense masses covering the intervals along the river, presented a curious spectacle.

City of Concord, New Hampshire

MALCOLM McLANE
MAYOR

March, 1970

Herbert E. Little, President
Merrimack County Savings Bank
Concord, New Hampshire

Dear Mr. Little:

May I express appreciation for your thoughtfulness in making available a reprint copy of the unique 1824 Annals of Concord for every family in the City.

This rare volume has become a virtually forgotten milestone in our heritage. I am sure its stirring depiction of the first century of our community's life will be thoroughly enjoyed by all who now have opportunity to share it.

Your institution is to be commended for this most unusual display of civic enterprise.

Sincerely yours,

Malcolm McLane

Mayor

www.ingramcontent.com/pod-product-compliance
Lightning Source LLC
Chambersburg PA
CBHW071137280326
41935CB00010B/1258